HOW SACRIFICE AND SERVICE
HELPED IN ACHIEVING MY DREAM
OF BECOMING A SURGEON

THROUGH
IT
ALL

A MEMOIR

GREGORY HILL, D.O.

DEDICATION

To my mother, Doretta L. Dunkley, a robust and smart taskmaster, who taught me always to do my best regardless of the job. She was supportive in every phase of my journey! In one of our final conversations, she reminded me of her favorite scripture: Proverbs 3:5-6, Trust in the Lord with all thine heart; and lean not unto thine own understanding. In all thy ways acknowledge him, and he shall direct thy paths. KJV

To my baby brother, Arthur (Artie) H. Dunkley, Sr., whom we lost during the writing of the book. You were gone too soon. I love you and miss you!

ACKNOWLEDGMENT

My wife Judi, an accomplished woman in her own right, is dedicated to ensuring we hear the voices of those who can't speak for themselves. Thank you for your listening ear and for providing wise counsel. Thank you for an incredible journey, making me laugh and keeping me grounded!

My children are Kristen, Brandon, Terrell, and Ariss. Thanks for your unconditional love and support.

My brother Jerry and sister-in-law Nikole have always been in my corner, regardless of the stage of my career. They have provided wisdom, motivation, and encouragement while writing this book. Thank You!

My sister Cindi, a gifted poet, has always supported her "big brother." Thank You!

My other siblings, John and Sharon, for their love and support.

Dr. Dale Okorodudu, the founder of Black Men in White Coats, physician, author, publisher, and book coach, reached out and asked the question have you ever thought about writing a book? Thank you for coaching and encouraging me to share my story.

Tammy Kling, author, publisher, and coach, thank you for sharing your wisdom about the new world of writing. Thank you for coaching with a servant spirit.

James Yarbrough for the cover design and Imani Womack for developing my website: drhill-inspiringandeducating.com, Thank You!

CONTENTS

INTRODUCTION

Young kids are often asked: 'What do you want to do when you grow up?'

It's an inevitable question asked by an aunt, uncle, or stranger, usually around the time a child graduates high school.

When I was young I often pondered that question, considering the options in my mind.

Will I be a doctor, lawyer, accountant or teacher? Will I make a lot of money? Will I save lives?

It can be an overwhelming season because it feels as if one is living in the in-between. Between your past and the future, with a large dose of uncertainty. We've all been there, and it's not fun!

One of the reasons I decided to share my story, is the feeling I had in the in-between. I wanted to reassure others who feel uncertain, scared, or stuck, that they really can move forward despite the uncertainty with the faith and hope that they can achieve their dreams!

In this book, I hope to empower, educate and enlighten others. Whether it be high school or college students, on the strategies for navigating their best life while preparing for the future. Also, I want to encourage every reader to understand that success WILL happen for you-- despite any personal, financial, social, and familial challenges.

Throughout my journey, I share the challenges of my background, including financial obstacles that made me doubt my ability to achieve my dream of becoming a medical doctor.

During that time of intense scrutiny and decision making, I faced people who let me know that they didn't believe in me. Some were subtle, and others were direct-- but I faced it.

Through it all, I became a successful board certified orthopedic surgeon with more than 30 years of experience as well as 23 years as a physician and surgeon in the U.S. Army Reserves and the Ohio Army National Guard. Personal challenges of divorce and an active duty deployment in the middle of a busy practice in support of Operation Iraqi Freedom following 9/11. This certainly created anxiety and stress for me and my family. *"Through it all,"* I managed to come out on top with family, practice and career. I really believe my deployment had a profound effect on my perspective of the world. You too will have challenges or situations that make you realize you must strive for excellence and there are no do-overs. Challenges present opportunities to learn and change your perspective on life. Perhaps you have lost a loved one, lost a job, or have significant financial issues. All of these situations will develop your character and make you stronger. In the morning, you will feel more energetic and ready to take on the world.

I was successful in becoming an orthopedic surgeon for more than 30 years and was a successful military surgeon in the Iraq war.

Anyone can be successful if they possess discipline, tenacity, and faith, and are prepared academically. You can beat the odds as I did and overcome the obstacles when they occur. How will you do it? You'll do it one day at a time, by tackling any challenge or adversity as they come.

In today's world we have an information highway with cell phones or handheld computers with immediate access to worldwide information. Google and the internet have changed the world and how we access information. When I talk to my grandkids about growing up, I tell them there was no internet, no Google and no cell phones. I commented, 'When we were young, cell phones were only for rich people.' They looked at me in amazement, laughed and replied, 'Wow, papa, you're just old.'

As a young student aspiring to become a medical doctor, certain factors allowed me to become successful and to work through various challenges in high school and college. The factors included **Faith**, **Leadership**, **Discipline**, **Grit and Mentoring!**

Grit is simply the willpower to keep pushing forward towards your goal, regardless of what others say or do. You have to do what you want despite the naysayers or those who put obstacles on your way-- to never lose sight of your dreams. Remaining rooted in Faith has helped me overcome adversity along the way. **Philippians 4:13**: *"I can do all things through Christ who strengthens me."* (KJV). This scripture has been one of my favorites since high school and has given me strength over and over during my life.

Maybe you have heard these comments: "I don't think you're college material; I'm not sure you can get into medical school," "How can you afford college?" These were some of the comments I heard, and some of the worst ones lived rent-free in my head.

When defeating words enter your mind, you have to take them captive instead of entertaining them. The biggest battle you may face in your lifetime is in your mind.

My mom would always share stories about growing up in the South during the 1940s and 50s, which definitely affected how she viewed the world from an African American perspective. I made the best of my circumstances, enduring the challenges of growing up in the inner city of Akron, Ohio during the turbulent 60s. Perhaps because I was so young I really didn't know what hard times were.

Months before my mom passed we had a conversation as we often would about her journey and challenges growing up in the South. In addition to life's wisdom she had a very good grasp of specific Bible verses and chapters. I asked her, 'Mom what is your favorite scripture?' She answered, 'Oh Gregory, you know **Proverbs 3:5-6** *'Trust in the Lord with all thine heart; and lean not unto thine own understanding. In all thy ways acknowledge him, and he shall direct thy path.'* (KJV)". When life becomes confusing, and I am not sure of the right choice for a particular situation, *Proverbs 3:5-6* is where I go for guidance to help me make the best decision! This process has always worked for me over and over again. I am blessed I had so much wisdom poured into me during my childhood that remains with me today. When times get tough, we all need wisdom and prayer to help us find the right answers to life's challenges. I never forgot those words Mom shared with me.

What's your favorite scripture? Do you have one? Your special verse will help you navigate a tough decision or situation in your life. If you don't have one yet, feel free to borrow my favorite.

One of the other important topics I comment on in the book is that of *Financial Literacy*. It is vitally important in nearly all aspects of our lives. Consider how will you pay for college, a car or a house. Financial literacy was not a "thing" when I grew up, at least not in most African American households. It is important to understand my parents never had investments and I'm sure they didn't have a 401K or an IRA. I think they had savings and checking accounts. I really hope the young people and adults who read this book will take away some of the information I was not exposed to as a child, particularly regarding financial literacy and better college preparation.

Later, I learned alcohol was present in our household. In my opinion, the situation created stress for me and my siblings (more about that later). **Faith, structure** and **discipline** had the largest impact on my success, character development and maturity. It's important to note achieving success is difficult without discipline, structure, and academic preparation. If you didn't have it as a child, now is the time to create it for yourself. Having good character is a choice, and so is creating a disciplined routine that helps you structure your life.

Most of the structure came from family discipline and attending church regularly.

Attending New Hope Baptist Church as a youngster is where I learned the importance of FAITH and LEADERSHIP. As a new member of my church, I was like other kids trying to figure it out. I just wanted to belong and be accepted by my friends. I kept hearing about faith and wanted to know how I could apply it to my life. I realized early on faith was a critical element required to navigate the challenges of financing and successfully graduating from college. I figured it took faith to believe my dream would come true despite various obstacles.

There will be times when the road is unclear, and you must lean on a higher power. This is when your faith is tested!

After graduating from high school, I needed money for college. So my training as a surgical tech and PA helped alleviate some of the financial burden on me since my parents were unable to pay for college. I was driven and needed to grow self-discipline too. No one has it easy during college, and my story is no different.

Frustrations were plentiful for me, particularly in the first couple of years of college. I signed up for Chemistry, Biology and Psychology. The Chemistry and Biology classes both had labs so essentially it seemed like there were 2 extra classes. The first quarter of college was extremely stressful primarily because this was a completely new experience. I was very concerned about my study habits. I would certainly suggest to young students they have good study habits before attending college. This would certainly make the transition from high school to college more tolerable and less stressful.

My life has centered around six key principles. These included *Faith, Perseverance, Relationships, Service, Preparation, and Discipline*. What principles do you want to claim for your life? It's never too early or too late to start thinking about them.

Today, my life of service extends beyond the operating room. As part of my efforts to give back to my community, I participated in several initiatives (including those held by my fraternity, *Phi*

Beta Sigma Fraternity, Inc., whose motto is culture for service and service for humanity). In addition, in 2022, I participated in the first-ever *Black Men in White Coats Youth Summit* in Akron. Ohio. This movement is designed to increase the visibility of black doctors to communities through exposure, inspiration, and mentoring. Many middle and high school students stated that they have never encountered a doctor who is black. So we think early exposure and early visibility can and will excite and motivate the next generation to become doctors. When President Obama became the first African-American president of the United States and Kamala Harris became the first African-American female to become Vice President of the United States, young African American students and other minorities were empowered to dream bigger and reach higher regarding their goals and aspirations. I think empowering young people with vital information about career choices, academics, and strategies for success will go a long way in helping them become successful wherever their journey takes them!

I wrote this book for students, young and old, who have doubts about their future. They may be faced with the lack of emotional and financial support, love and other challenges or perhaps they have all of that--but a lack of self-discipline. I hope you enjoy my journey!

CHAPTER ONE
THE EARLY YEARS

In the early years, we lived in the public housing projects on the west side of Akron, Ohio called Edgewood Homes. I lived with my mom and two siblings. I was the oldest, was born in 1956; my sister, Gwendolyn (Cindi), was born in 1959, and my brother Jerry born in 1964.Akron, at that time, was a medium-sized city in Ohio with a population near 200,000.Historically, in the 60s the city was known as the "rubber capital of the world" because of the number of Rubber Companies in the city. These companies included *The Goodrich Tire Co., The Goodyear Tire and Rubber Company, The Firestone Rubber Company and The General Tire Company.* In addition, *Quaker Oats* was headquartered in Akron as well. Yes, it was the company that made oatmeal. Over the last 20 years, Akron has become a center for polymer research and development that is globally recognized. In addition, the rubber companies have transferred production overseas or to the south where the production costs are lower and unions are not as strong. *The Goodyear Tire and*

Rubber Company and The Bridgestone Company have retained their corporate headquarters in Akron.

My fondest memories of living in Akron occurred during the tumultuous 60s when civil unrest was common. We lived on Edgewood Avenue across the street from the Akron Zoo. We made friends and played in Perkins Park which was an area adjacent to the Akron Zoo. Perkins Park had a baseball diamond, tennis courts and Indian trails for hiking. In the summertime the city of Akron would have programs for the kids who lived in Edgewood homes and the surrounding areas. We participated in crafts, softball, tennis and pool. The best times occurred during the summer when the community would frequent the "Custard Stand" a local gem that made the best foot long Coney dogs, hamburgers and ice cream. Car enthusiasts would also bring their fancy cars for everyone to view. During the winters we had plenty of snow and hills for sled riding and snowballs. My siblings and I would play outside in the snow for hours and hours till our hands were numb. Once we went inside to warm them up, we would cry when we ran water on our hands to warm them up. My dad would exclaim, "Why in the hell would you stay outside in the cold till your hands hurt!"

I thought Akron was a safe place until one day while watching the news there was a report of a dead woman found in the wading pool at Perkins Woods Park near the Akron Zoo. Following the news report of the identification of the body, I noticed the police coming to our next-door neighbor's apartment to arrest the woman's husband. I thought, "Oh My God! did this really happen in our neighborhood?" These types of occurrences were rare to say the least.

Family

My mother, Doretta L. Dunkley was a divorced single mom. She was born in Talladega, Alabama and had 4 other siblings. She was raised by her grandmother because her mom was always working. All of the kids lived on the farm with their grandmother and grandfather. My mom told us life was pretty tough due to racism and living in the South. This was during the *Jim Crow era* which was the establishment and enforcement of racial segregation. The time frame for *"Jim Crow"* was from 1865-1960s. Formal and informal segregation policies were present in other areas of the country even if some of the areas were outside the South. For example there were separate drinking fountains and bathrooms for whites and blacks. This was the way of life for my mom during her early years in Alabama. According to my mom, as a child, she excelled academically and received straight A's until she became severely ill at age 8 or 9. She developed Scarlet Fever, became comatose and was near death. Mom was unconscious for about 3 weeks before she regained consciousness. There were no traditional physical therapy programs to assist with her rehabilitation. All of her rehabilitation was done at home by her family. She eventually became stronger and returned to school. Following intense therapy at home, she regained her strength, learned to walk again and finally returned to school. Upon graduation from high school, she enrolled at Talladega College to study education. The stress of college caused her to drop out after one year. The financial burden on her parents and grandparents was beyond their ability to support her through college. After an unsuccessful year in college, she returned to Talladega, met and married James A. Hill and moved to Akron, Ohio around 1951. I was born January 30, 1956 at Akron City Hospital where I would later work to gain valuable experience and the money to support my undergraduate education.

They were married for about 8 years before they divorced. After her divorce, John Dunkley Sr. entered the picture and would later become my stepfather. He had 2 children, John Jr. and Sharon, from his previous marriage. John Jr. was approximately 1 1/2 years older than me and Sharon and I were close in age. They would come over on weekends to spend time with our family. Times were more fun when John and Sharon came over. My younger sister Gwendolyn (Cindi) was three years younger than me but always wanted to hang out with the older siblings. She was a bit precocious, bright, energetic and always wanted to do things by herself. When I was 9 years old, one of my memorable moments was walking my sister to school, who was 6 years old. My sister thought she could walk to school by herself. I wanted to walk with the boys in the neighborhood. My next-door neighbor, Renee said she would walk my sister to school. Well, my sister thought she could cross the street by herself and was hit by a car. She sustained significant injuries which landed her in Akron Children's Hospital. She sustained a fractured femur and multiple abrasions. She spent several days in traction at the hospital and remained in a Hip Spica Cast for 6 weeks. I was so afraid of the outcome of the accident. My first thought centered on her injuries and whether she would be okay. My second thought was whether my mother was going to severely discipline me. The answer to the second thought was YES! As I sat in Mrs. Klein's 4th grade classroom at Lane Elementary School, I was on pins and needles as you can imagine. A knock on the door interrupted her class and as Mrs. Klein began to talk to the lady at the door, I realized it was my mother and I thought "I'm going to die." Mrs. Klein pointed to me and said, "Gregory, your mother is here." I walked out with my mother and there was silence between the two of us until we got into the car. Once in the car, she told me about my sister's condition and said she would be alright. I felt a sigh of relief following the comment she would be okay. But I knew there was more to the story. Then came another lecture on disobedience! You can't imagine the number of lectures on disobedience that were given. My mom said we would have further discussion at home about the situation. She said she was going to do the talking and I was going to do the listening. Needless to say I had a "come to Jesus meeting" with my mother for disobeying her instructions. Many of you may have heard the term *"spare the rod and spoil the child."* Following the "come to Jesus meeting" with mom, she did not spare the rod. Once again she reinforced the need to always take care of my younger siblings regardless of what I wanted to do. My sister's injuries were all healed well without any long term sequelae. Cindi was always independent and actually moved out on her own at age 18 before graduating from high school. Naturally, we were all concerned about her moving out but her resilience and tenacity allowed her to survive on her own at 18 years of age and complete school on time.

Jerry was the next sibling after Cindi. He was eight years younger than me. He was smart and active in sports when he became a teenager. Jerry was a very good student, received excellent grades and was also very active in our church. My sister would read to him at a very early age which I think was the foundation for him to become a voracious reader. I became his advisor regarding education and a career path. I would talk to him regularly about his dreams and applying for scholarships to attend college. In no uncertain terms, I told him mom and dad could not afford to send him to college and the best way to leave Akron was to attend college by receiving academic scholarships and/or joining the military. I was so impressed when he was applying to colleges. Jerry received academic scholarships as well as the required congressional nomination to support his packet for applying to West Point Military Academy. He was accepted to the West Point Prep School at Fort Monmouth, New Jersey. The prep school is for students with a strong admission packet but may need additional preparation before going to the regular academy. There were insurmountable challenges at the prep school requiring Jerry to withdraw. He returned to Akron dejected, frustrated and wondering what was next for him. Leaving the prep school was emotionally draining for Jerry but our mom showed no sympathy. She asked him, "Now, what is your plan?" He never responded but was home about one week before enlisting in the Navy. After one year in prep school, he enlisted in the Navy and served 20 years before retiring in 2003 while serving in Iraq. While in the Navy, he completed his undergraduate degree and some of his graduate studies. Since he retired from the Navy, he has completed 2 Master's Degrees. Jerry is certainly accomplished academically and now is a Government and History teacher at Granby High School in Norfolk, Virginia. He is extremely passionate and committed about his role as a teacher at Granby High School. On occasion, while teaching his class, he will tell his students he has a brother who is a physician in Akron. The students express their disbelief because we are from Akron, Ohio. He will call me during one of his classes and ask me to share information with his students about education and my journey to becoming a physician. I am always excited to share a portion of my journey with them emphasizing all things are possible if they believe, prepare, have discipline and seize the opportunity when it presents itself! He had previously told them he was from Akron, Ohio and there were more successful people from Akron, other than basketball player, Lebron James. A professional athlete or rapper is often a source of success for students because of what they see on TV or online. To prove his point, he gave the students an exercise and asked them to Google my name and once they did, they found a picture of me in a white coat and said, "Mr. Jerry, he looks just like you but he has a different last name." He explained we were raised together and had the same mother but different fathers.

Our baby brother Arthur (Artie) was born in 1971 and he was 15 years younger than me, 7 years younger than Jerry and 12 years younger than my sister "Cindi". I think because of our age difference, there was a disconnect between us. Our siblings were a bit jealous because as the youngest, he was able to stay out late. He got his first car when he was 16 and played football and baseball all four years of high school. He lived a carefree life while in high school. He played on the high school football team, which won back-to-back state championships in 1988 and 89. I often said there seemed to be a lack of discipline in the household once the other siblings moved out. While I was in medical school I came home one weekend and asked mom, "Where is Artie?" She responded, "I do not know. I think he is someplace out in the streets" and I quickly responded, "We were never able to just hang out in the streets." We always had a curfew time to be home and always had to let our parents know the details of where we were going and with whom. Most of the time, we had to ask permission to go to the park, ride our bikes or visit friends. She later responded that she was tired of raising children and that the older siblings had actually taken all of her energy. Mom always had her hands full with the kids. She was a disciplinarian, always questioning, teaching and setting expectations. Following graduation from high school, Artie served four years in the United States Army and four years in the reserves. After his discharge from the military, he worked at the United States Postal Service for several years. Shortly after returning to Akron, he asked me about getting married. I shared he needed a little more time to acclimate to being discharged from the military. Following our initial conversation, a friend and I met Artie at a local wing place to give him wise counsel about waiting to get married. We were unsuccessful and he soon married his high school sweetheart Alecia Colvin who was also a member at New Hope Baptist Church. They had 2 children, Arthur Howard Dunkley Jr. and Kierra Dunkley. Unfortunately, Artie and Alecia divorced after about 2-3 years of marriage. Their divorce was amicable. Artie was always the life of the party and looked forward to holidays when he could show off his grilling talents. He learned to grill and cook from our mom who was a superb cook.

Alcohol and Addiction

For my readers, I want to share some pertinent family history that will provide a unique perspective on alcohol, addiction and its effect on our family.

Unfortunately, we lost our mother in March of 2016 from chronic cardiovascular and pulmonary issues and following her death Artie began consuming alcohol at an alarming rate. We (the family) thought he was depressed but he denied it and said he didn't need counseling. Our family concluded he was unable to grieve my mother's death. He refused to seek professional help regarding his mental health and began to have chronic medical issues related to chronic alcohol abuse. He developed avascular necrosis of both hips which required bilateral hip replacements (directly related to alcohol use). Avascular necrosis is a condition in which the blood supply to the femur is affected and the hips begin to collapse. There is severe pain with walking and prolonged standing. In addition to the hip issues, he began to have chronic cardiovascular problems, and liver and kidney issues. Finally, during the pandemic in 2020, he called me to say he was willing to go to rehab at the Louis Stokes Veteran's Administration Center in Cleveland. He was there for about 6-8 weeks and while there he contracted COVID. He didn't consume any alcohol and appeared to make good progress; however, prior to discharge, he stated he was going to get a drink on his way home. So, this really showed me the strength of his addiction. He began to have more frequent medical issues requiring acute hospitalization. Unfortunately, we lost him during the writing of this book in April 2023. While growing up our family always seemed to socialize and have a good time. There seemed to be a party on most weekends. By party, I mean music, food and alcohol. The parties seemed to be enjoyable. Despite not drinking as a youngster, my parents seemed to drink excessively. But what did I know? After a period of "partying," my parent's personalities seemed to change. Arguing, fussing, and domestic violence were all part of the situation. The more my parents argued, the more stress the kids faced, and this caused depression and anxiety. While in high school, I became quiet and withdrawn but was able to confide in one of my teachers in high school who suspected something was wrong at home. Nothing really changed at home after talking to my teacher except I felt better by sharing my feelings and frustration. At age 17 I thought I felt comfortable talking to my parents after they would always encourage me to share my feelings. They would say, "Gregory, you can always talk to mom and dad." So on a Sunday after church I planned to share feelings about their partying and drinking. I started the story by saying I loved them both and went into the details of my feelings. I said, "When we get together as a family we have the best time until the alcohol comes out and then there is arguing and fussing." They seemed to listen but at the end of our meeting I was told, "Our drinking is a grown-up thing and it has nothing to do with you." Needless to say I was frustrated and felt I had wasted my time and energy. Alcohol was always present in our household, and as I got older, I also came to the realization that my parents had alcohol addiction issues. However, while in high school I was in denial they were alcoholics because they both went to work daily and seemed to be responsible parents. Images of alcoholics on T.V. were depicted as derelicts, jobless or homeless. I became more informed and educated about addiction issues with alcohol and other substances. I believe my youngest brother received early exposure to alcohol which caused major long-term health issues for him. For our readers, please note many of you may have families who have addiction issues with alcohol and/or drugs. These complex issues can affect children's personalities, academic performance in school and their social and psychological development. I believe surrounding yourself with good people and a good church home may alleviate some of the stress associated with addiction. Connection groups and high school sports are both possible outlets for sharing your feelings and at times, frustration. Although alcohol is ever-present and responsible consumption can occur, new street drugs out there have proven to be deadly regardless of age, sex and race.

The new substance in the news is fentanyl, which is a highly potent synthetic opioid drug primarily used as an analgesic in a hospital setting. Fentanyl is 50 -100 times more potent than morphine. It is typically used in surgical settings and also in pain management for cancer patients. However, the drug is now on the streets and is often mixed with other drugs to enhance the effect. Often, those who purchase drugs on the streets are unaware fentanyl has been laced with pills or marijuana, leading to an overdose and subsequent death. One of the issues I feel compelled to comment on is marijuana. Many of our readers have been exposed to marijuana in one way or another, either at home, school or with friends. Over the last 20 years marijuana use has been consistent and now every state has laws concerning the uses of medical marijuana. Roughly two-thirds of the U.S. states have legalized the use of medical cannabis. In some states there is new proposed legislation for its recreational use. Some of the most common medical reasons cited are nausea and vomiting related to chemotherapy for cancer, migraine headaches and anxiety disorders. Another common medical use is for patients with severe forms of epilepsy. There are also medical marijuana dispensaries going up in our communities and it seems there is increased access to marijuana THC-related products such as gummies. THC or tetrahydrocannabinol is the chemical responsible for marijuana's mood-altering effects. Some of these gummies may be laced with other products and there may not be strict regulations on production and dispensing. The increased use of medical and recreational marijuana has become a source of significant revenue for those entrepreneurs. Please note for our readers: Marijuana and related products are still classified as Hallucinogens and there are examples of "bad trips" or severe hallucinations following the use of so-called minimal THC products.

A New Community

Life went on and our family eventually moved from the projects to West Akron, affectionately known as West Hill. We had a new house, a new school and a new community of friends. Once again tragedy struck our country. In the spring of April 1968, civil rights leader and activist Martin Luther King was assassinated and our country was in an uproar. Demonstrations, marches and rioting occurred in Akron and most major urban cities like Chicago, Detroit, New York and Los Angeles. Just as the violence subsided Senator Robert F. Kennedy was also assassinated and the demonstrations and violence returned. This was all new to me. Our neighborhoods were more prone to curfews, restrictions, and police presence than usual. Eventually the violence calmed down and things returned to normal.

The new schools were fun and uncomfortable all at the same time. Meeting new friends at times created anxiety but most of the time it was fun playing baseball, basketball and football with the neighborhood guys. There was minor bullying present but nothing like it is today. Most disagreements were settled outside of school or simply ignored.

In high school, students were trying to find their own identity, make new friends and become comfortable in the new environment. I was interested in sports but as the oldest sibling I had to be home to watch my brothers and sisters. We had a new addition to our family, Arthur or Artie was born in 1971. So, now we had a full house of siblings with me, Cindy, Jerry, John, Arthur and Sharon and it was so much fun especially on Sunday mornings at breakfast before he went to church. Before church our dad and the brothers would deliver newspapers at 4 AM for the Akron Beacon Journal. After the newspaper deliveries, we went to a famous local spot known as Krispy Kreme Donuts. Their donuts were absolutely the best in Akron. We stood in line waiting for a sample donut while we placed our orders. These experiences contributed to my fondest memories growing up and I still frequent this place for donuts.

NOTES

CHAPTER TWO

CHURCH AND LEADERSHIP

We did not attend church regularly until my stepdad's mother passed away. She was affectionately known as "Big Mama," and we would see her nearly every Sunday while she was in a nursing home. Our family started attending church regularly after her passing. In those days, the typical African-American family would attend church following the leadership of the father. My parents became active in the church. My dad became a deacon, and my mother a deaconess. These were highly respected leadership positions in our church.

I committed my life to Christ around the age of 15 or 16 and soon thereafter, Jerry, Cindi and Artie joined. John and Sharon didn't join then because they only came over every couple of weeks. They would later join New Hope Baptist Church as well. At that time, New Hope Baptist Church was a small missionary Baptist Church on the Eastside of Akron composed primarily of relatives of the Flinn, Drake families and other large families.

Our pastor, the Rev. John H. Flinn, was an excellent leader and pastor. Pastor Flinn eventually baptized all of my siblings. As our church grew, we needed more space and we began a project to build a new church on the Westside of Akron. The location of the new church was actually very close to our home. The time to church was a 5-minute car ride or 15 to 20-minute walk. There were expectations of new members to join one of the sections at New Hope. These sections included joining the choir, Sunday school, the Usher board, or the security team. I became active and joined the Sunday school and the choir. This meant I had to attend church during the week on Thursdays for choir rehearsal. In the Sunday school I was appointed the position of the assistant superintendent. As the assistant superintendent, my responsibility was to organize the classes and lead the Sunday school lessons in the absence of the superintendent. I believe my involvement in Sunday school provided the principles of leadership, modeling, and public speaking. In our home church, it was customary for members to publicly declare their faith through a 'testimony'. I truly believe my early involvement in the church provided the template for public speaking and being comfortable speaking in front of large groups. One of my classes during my first quarter in college was effective communications which focused on public speaking. I felt very comfortable in that class and wondered why others were stressed by speaking before small or large groups.

Additional church involvement included performing the church welcome engagements and organizing youth meetings. I attended national youth conferences which showed young people how to become engaged in church and what leadership and responsibility meant for them.

For our readers, I believe local involvement in organizations at your high school or community center will provide early exposure for modeling leadership, public speaking and service. These early experiences will provide a template for your success in college, graduate school and your career regardless of your profession. Hopefully, that template will reinforce your confidence and belief that you can be successful in whatever you choose.

High School

I attended John R. Buchtel High School which was an inner-city high school with a racial makeup of approximately 50-50. I enrolled in college prep classes as well as vocational classes. In tenth grade our high school started a new vocational program called Medical Careers. I was intrigued by this new program which I thought was the best of both worlds. How could you lose? The purpose of this program was to equip students with healthcare vocational training which provided them with hospital skills suitable for employment following graduation from high school. Students would have options of going directly to work or attending college or both. The requirements included good grades and completion of core academic classes. The first year academic classes of the program consisted of basic sciences such as Anatomy and Physiology, Chemistry, Medical Terminology and Physics. The second year of the program consisted of 1/2 day of clinical training of your choice at the hospital and the other half day at your high school for your regular class work. Clinical training options included operating room technology, respiratory therapy, physical therapy assisting, nursing and x-ray technology. In the 10th grade of the program, students took a tour to Akron City Hospital to observe surgeries, visit the emergency room, physical therapy and other departments to provide exposure and in general get an idea of what specialty interested us. A significant point in my life occurred when I visited the operating room at Akron City Hospital and was completely intrigued and excited about observing a surgery. It was then I had an epiphany and decided that I wanted to become a surgeon. From that moment on I became more focused and passionate about my education. There would be challenges that came up that I hadn't anticipated. These challenges included getting into college and how to pay for it. The first challenge had to do with the college entrance exam. None of our counselors had ever talked about college entrance exams let alone going to college. It seemed to me my guidance counselor casually mentioned if I had plans on attending college I would need to take the SAT or the ACT. These were the Scholastic Aptitude Test and the American College Test. Both of these tests are meant to measure your readiness for college based on what you have learned in school. I had concerns about the exam, including strategies for preparing and succeeding on it. I remember my counselor telling me, "Don't be anxious because there's no way you can actually study for the exam. Generally, it is an accumulation of what you already know." He instructed me to get to the University of Akron on Saturday morning and register for the exam. He stated the exam would take approximately 4 to 5 hours and our school would receive my results. I felt uneasy about preparing for the exam and taking the exam since no one from an educational standpoint had ever commented about it. Well, just as you would imagine I followed up with the guidance counselor after taking the exam and he said I did not perform very well on the test and based on the analysis of the results I should attend college. I was so upset by these comments and began to ask the question for example "How can I perform well on the test when I do not feel I was given proper instructions?" I then asked a follow up question, "How can one stupid test determine what I will be in the future?" My counselor never said "I could retake the exam or take a prep course." Later, I found out that one of the high schools in Northwest Akron, Firestone High school had received early instruction about the examination as well as opportunities to retake the exam. Immediately, I felt that this was an injustice because we were an inner-city school and no one really cared about our education following high school. Later I learned that this was a common practice in the 70s and it was termed "academic steering". Apparently, in speaking to other successful classmates, they were also told that they did not have the academic fortitude or the aptitude to be successful in college and that most likely "we" would be successful with highly technical jobs. Most of the women were told they would be better suited as secretaries, teachers or nurses' aides. This incensed me and gave me more energy and passion to strive for my goal of becoming a doctor.

The other challenge had to do with finances. I spoke to my mother about going to college and expressed my interest in attending Howard University in Washington DC. With a surprised look on her face, she said, "Howard University, you mean that black school in Washington DC?" I responded, "Yes! I think it would be wonderful to attend a Historically Black College or University (HBCU)" She quickly responded, "We don't have money for that university and we barely have money for you to attend the University of Akron." She went on to say, "I think we can help you pay for one-quarter of college and then you are on your own. We think the best way for you to do this is through grants, loans and scholarships." Once again, I felt as though I was at a disadvantage compared to other students. But this also gave me motivation and passion and set me on a path to pursue my goal of becoming a physician and surgeon.

College Years

Like many other students, I enrolled in the University of Akron majoring in Pre-Med and Biology. Yes, I received student loans, grants and some scholarships. I felt college classes were challenging and my first quarter classes were Biology, Chemistry, Psychology and English. I passed all of my classes in my first quarter of college but was not satisfied with my grades overall. In 1974 I began working at Akron City Hospital as a surgical tech. I was so excited about my new job with a starting salary of $2.79 per hour. I thought I had finally arrived having my own money and a car. My mother insisted I pay rent for living at home. She said I couldn't live anywhere for the amount she charged me. The amount covered my meals, lodging and laundry. Ultimately, it proved to be a very good deal.

It was an incredible experience working side-by-side with wonderful surgeons, nurses and other staff members. They were very motivating, encouraging and urging me to continue in college and pursue my dream of becoming a physician.

Akron City Hospital was a level 1 trauma center and we treated all kinds of injuries including fractures, motor vehicle accidents, gunshot wounds and any patients needing tertiary care. Working there provided exposure to a variety of surgical cases that would ultimately benefit me in my future training.

That is where I met Hand Surgeon Dr. Frank Forshew and Obstetrician and Gynecologist Dr. Milton Hamblin. These gentlemen would later become my mentors. Drs. Hamblin, Forshew and other surgeons at the hospital consistently encouraged me and provided very valuable information regarding classes, strategies and other pointers to enhance my probability of getting accepted into medical school. I originally met Dr. Hamblin through my mother who was one of his patients. He was quiet, soft-spoken and an excellent surgeon and shared his insight on what classes to take while in college. Dr. Forshew was equally quiet and a gifted surgeon. Many of the cases he performed were complex hand injuries. I had the opportunity to scrub (pass instruments) and assist with a number of those procedures. Hence, I actually spent quite a bit of time with him while I was a surgical tech at Akron City Hospital while completing my undergraduate Pre-Med classes.

I was busy with classes, working and trying to maintain a social life. I became frustrated with Pre-Med and questioned whether I should change my major or work part-time where I could really focus on my academics. My mother would repeatedly say I had too many irons in the fire. I remember the following comment from my mother: "Gregory, you're smart but NOT that damn smart." You need to prepare your mind and focus on your work and studies if you want to become a doctor".

After 3 frustrating years at the University of Akron, I made decided to transfer to Cuyahoga Community College (CCC) in Parma, Ohio to study to become a Surgical Physician Assistant. I felt studying Surgical Physicians Assisting would give me a fresh start and backup plan in the event I did not get accepted to medical school. The program consisted of more science courses including Surgical Anatomy and Physiology, suturing and splinting and casting, general assisting in surgery and the office. The experience was wonderful and restored my confidence in my test taking and my overall confidence. It also restored my faith that I had the potential to do well in medical school if only given the opportunity. While at CCC I continued to work at Akron City Hospital on weekends and holidays to make money for school. I graduated with honors at Cuyahoga Community College and was offered a position as a Surgical PA but decided to complete my Pre-Med Studies in Biology and Allied Health at Baldwin Wallace College in Berea, Ohio.

Faith

While at Baldwin Wallace College, I lived on campus during the week. On weekends I would drive to Akron, where I would work Friday evening, Saturday and Sunday and then return to Berea for classes on Monday morning. I thoroughly enjoyed my experience at Baldwin Wallace College participating in student life and campus activities, joining a fraternity and attending sporting events. In addition, I was happy with my academic performance at Baldwin Wallace College. I felt more mature, focused and motivated about applying to medical school. I knew Baldwin Wallace College (University) was a special place. Once I was accepted to Baldwin Wallace College University I was contacted by the Chair of the Biology Department, Donald Dean, Ph.D. He called me on a Sunday afternoon to welcome me to the college and told me he was excited to have me as a student there. Also, I had a wonderful advisor at Baldwin Wallace named Stephen Hilliard, Ph.D. He was always supportive, available, and provided up-to-date information about the application process to medical school. He was the first person to talk to me about an osteopathic medical school.

He told me that there was a new medical school at Ohio University (OU) in Athens, Ohio but it was an osteopathic medical school. I said I don't know much about osteopathic medical schools but I heard of osteopathic doctors (D.O.'s) at Akron City Hospital. He went on to say, "They're recruiting qualified minority students and I think you certainly qualify and we should take a road trip to Athens, Ohio to visit the Ohio University College of Osteopathic Medicine School (now Ohio University Heritage College of Osteopathic Medicine)" I thought "Oh my God! can this really be happening?" So we packed our bags and drove to Ohio University College of Osteopathic Medicine. Essentially, this was Ohio University's opportunity to showcase their campus, and discuss their program and admission requirements. While at OU, Dr. Hilliard stated I certainly met the qualifications and he thought I would do well here. I was so excited about the opportunity to attend Ohio University College of Osteopathic Medicine but then I thought how can I afford to attend medical school if I am accepted? Later, I was informed that the initial step is to enroll in medical school and the next step is to determine how to pay for it. One of the requirements for admission to Ohio University College of

Osteopathic Medicine was a letter from a "D.O." One of my best friends from BW was Shelly Glover who was also a Biology major. While discussing admission to Osteopathic medical schools with Shelly, she mentioned "My dad is a D.O. and he went to Philadelphia College of Osteopathic Medicine." I told myself, "Oh my, if I could only meet Dr. Glover and get a letter of recommendation I would be one step closer to my dream of becoming a doctor." Shelly introduced me to Dr. Glover and I told him I was applying to Ohio University College of Osteopathic Medicine. Dr. Glover graciously agreed to write a letter of recommendation for me. He also gave me pointers on how to prepare for the interview and how to be successful in medical school.

While I was excited about the opportunity to apply to Ohio University and other medical schools, I received some surprising information from my girlfriend in Akron. She stated she was pregnant and I was going to be a father. I quickly thought what will I do? Will I get married and quit school or will I go to medical school or will I do both? The situation became very stressful and ultimately I became the father of my daughter, Kristen L. Johnson. But more surprising was my relationship with her mother, Kathy. It was very strained and stressful. Following lengthy conversations, we ultimately decided marriage was not in the cards for us. It also became more challenging to see my daughter and be a good dad. Despite the new situation of becoming a father, I decided to still pursue my dream of becoming a physician. Later, I met a young lady, Sharon Williams in my college Spanish class at the University of Akron who also worked at Akron City Hospital.

We began to date and ultimately married in July 1983 following my first year of medical school. Interestingly, Sharon had a son Terrell and we immediately had a blended family. As I prepared for the second year of medical school, Sharon visited Athens Ohio but was unable to find employment. She remained in Akron where she continued to work at Akron City Hospital. I came home at regular intervals to see Sharon and my kids. Following the conclusion of the second year of medical school I was fortunate to have my clinical rotations in Columbus, Ohio. My family was able to move to Columbus while I completed my third and fourth year clinical rotations.

CHAPTER THREE

GAP YEAR AND SURGICAL EXPERIENCE

In 1981, I graduated from Baldwin Wallace College with an undergraduate degree in Biology and Allied Health. I had plans to take a year off from school, which is known as a gap year. This allowed me to take a break, reorganize, and possibly find employment while applying to medical school. Shortly after graduation I received a phone call from my mentor Dr. Frank Forshew and there was excitement in his voice. He said, "Congratulations on finishing your Pre-Med requirements and I understand you are going to apply to medical school." I responded in the affirmative, and he went on to say I understand you are taking a year off from school. I would like to offer you a position on our surgical team during your year off. I said, "But you understand I will be leaving after 1 year to attend school." He said it doesn't matter because I think this will be a wonderful opportunity for you and you will be a great asset to our team. Immediately, I said yes and told him I would be honored to be a part of his surgical team. I put in my resignation at Akron City

Hospital and then began to work with Dr. Forshew as his personal surgical PA in the office and the operating room.

When I began my work with Dr. Forshew, I was so humbled and excited to work side by side with him in the office and surgery. I learned how to interview patients, apply splints and casts, and assist with complex orthopedic and microsurgical cases. In the OR I worked side by side with the orthopedic residents and attended their educational conferences as well. The year with Dr. Forshew provided a wonderful educational, clinical and professional experience. The clinical experience provided a wonderful introduction to hand surgery and proved to be beneficial to my career choice of becoming an orthopedic hand surgeon. Professionally, I was also able to talk with Dr. Forshew about his medical school experience and what I could expect going to medical school. He said, "It would be the best and the worst time of your life." He referred to the hard work of long study hours, and challenging exams but at the same time meeting lifelong friends, great professors and having great experiences.

Application to Medical School

During the gap year, I applied to several medical schools in Ohio and a few on the West Coast and Pennsylvania. Applying to medical school is very stressful, and one can typically expect denials or rejections for admission. I was fortunate to have several interviews including Northeast Medical University

(NEOMED) in Rootstown, Ohio; Wright State University in Dayton, Ohio; Medical College of Ohio in Toledo and Ohio University College of Osteopathic Medicine in Athens, Ohio. The interview at NEOMED was not friendly, the faculty seemed cold, the students were distant and I was not impressed. Needless to say I was not accepted to NEOMED. Both of the interviews at Wright State and Medical College of Ohio went very well and I was impressed with the faculty, facility and students. During the interview at the Medical College of Ohio, I met one of the physiology professors, Barry Richardson, Ed.D. I had previously met Dr. Richardson at the University of Akron.

During my interview I was pleased to see a familiar face. We had a very in-depth meaningful conversation. He seemed to know something I didn't. He asked the question "What happens if you get in the D.O. school and you're on the waiting list at one of the allopathic schools?" He must have known something I didn't. Ultimately, I ended up on the waiting list at the Medical College of Ohio in Toledo and Wright State Medical School in Dayton but needed to interview at Ohio University COM.

The interview at OU went very well overall despite one faculty member's negative comments about my qualifications. When I arrived at his office it smelled of pipe tobacco and as the interviewer proceeded to review my file, there was pipe tobacco scattered about his desk. It appeared he was unprepared and was reviewing my file at the very last minute. Following his comments regarding my qualifications I responded, "Thank you for your time but I WILL BE successful!"

The admission committee met following my interview and the decision was made to offer me admission to Ohio University College of Osteopathic Medicine. It was a wonderful day receiving the phone call from Ed Beckett, Dean of admissions from the college. I still remember the words he said, "Greg, this is Ed Beckett from Ohio University and the admissions committee met and we want to offer you a position in next year's class. Now I'm sure you have other interviews but if you want us to hold a spot for you-- we need $100." I said, "Yes sir, thank you and I will send the money in." Once again I felt my faith had sustained me and now I will be able to pursue my dream of becoming a surgeon despite several obstacles. Those included a negative opinion from my high school counselors, poor performance on the ACT, lack of funding to complete college in 4 years and the negative opinion by one of the faculty at Ohio University College of Osteopathic Medicine.

The Medical School Experience: "Becoming a Bobcat"

I moved to Athens before classes started and moved into The College Inn, a private dormitory on campus. The medical students were housed on one floor and the engineering students were on another floor. I attended the meet and greet picnic the weekend before classes started. While at the picnic, I had the opportunity to meet faculty advisors and classmates. What a wonderful experience to be a part of the class of 1986! But I felt a little uneasy about being there. There were 100 students in our class and only 4 African American students. On the first day of class, we sat in the auditorium in Irvine Hall and one of the faculty members said, "Welcome to Ohio University College of Osteopathic Medicine, class of 1986. You can now relax and there is no further need for competition. You are the best of the best." Next he says, "Look to your left and your right. One of you may not be here at the end of the year." Of course this created additional stress on most of the students. Well, Dr. Forshew was right! It was the best and the worst of times. Following the first 2 years of medical school the decision is made regarding the location of our clinical rotations. At that time I had a resurgence of concerns about performing well in the hospital setting. Because of those concerns and the need to compete, I was very driven to be one of the best students at my clinical rotation site. One of my most challenging issues of the first quarter was time management and how to handle the stress of medical school and learn to relax. Most of the students had similar issues but most of us eventually acclimated to classes, exams, anatomy labs and the smell of the preservative formalin. Our schedules were rigorous but I was stressed and excited at the same time. Since I worked in surgery, I quickly gravitated to the Anatomy lab and became the main dissector of the cadaver at our table. Anatomy was my best subject and this was because of the 8 years of surgical experience prior to going to medical school. Biochemistry was probably the most challenging class of the first quarter because some of the concepts seemed foreign to me. Biochemistry was one of the few classes that I did not take as an undergraduate at Baldwin Wallace College. I had to retake the final exam at the end of the first quarter over the Christmas break. I passed the exam without problems and prepared for the winter quarter. One of the things that I noticed in medical school was there was always this subtle competition for the top grades in a given subject. Our teachers and professors often emphasize "merely pass the test" but it seemed the students were all very driven and competed on all levels. To me this all makes sense since we were in professional school studying to become physicians.

An example of this stress occurred following exams when the test scores were placed on the outside of a classroom by the last 4 digits of our social security number. Following the announcement the scores were in, students congregated around the wall trying to see their scores, often commenting about the number of scores above and below the passing line. Ultimately, most students became comfortable with the process of taking exams. It was very important to learn what worked best for the individual students regarding managing their stress. We had a few students who openly stated there was no time for outside activities like movies, dating or eating out but only time to study to get the best grades. Unfortunately, one of the top students in the sophomore year who made those comments began to have headaches which required him to be on medication. The side effects of the medication caused drowsiness and he ultimately dropped out of school because of health reasons. Many of our classmates often wondered whether the stress of medical school ultimately caused the headaches that made him resign from school. During the winter or spring of the first year, I became more comfortable in class and was able to manage the stress of medical school. My method of managing stress included regular working-outs, playing basketball and socializing with my classmates.

Recently, I had a conversation with my brother Jerry about my medical school experience. He asked me, "At any point in your medical school journey or thereafter did you have concerns regarding your confidence about completing medical school?" My response was, "Absolutely I had concerns about my confidence." However, this was early in the medical school process and specifically I had issues following the end of the first quarter.

In the spring of our freshman year, we had a hospital fair where hospitals from the region would set up tables to provide information regarding internships and residencies. In addition, there were several military organizations present including the United States Army, Army Reserves, Ohio National Guard, United States Navy and the United States Air Force. They all provided information regarding military medical scholarships, educational opportunities and careers in the military.

At the hospital fair I had the opportunity to speak with Colonel Aaron Warren of the Ohio Army National Guard. I was impressed with his uniform, his presentation and the training opportunities provided by joining the United States Army Reserves and the National Guard. He was a physician in the Medical Corps of the Ohio Army National Guard and was responsible for recruiting new medical students to the organization. The opportunity appeared to be a win-win for me and The Army National Guard because of the opportunity to obtain an excellent military medical education as well as receive credit for clinical rotations while on active duty. As a junior and senior medical student, I was afforded the opportunity of rotations at some of the nation's best military hospitals which included Brooke Army Medical Center in San Antonio, Texas, Walter Reed Army Hospital in Washington DC, and William Beaumont Army Medical Center in El Paso, Texas as well as many others.

In March 1983, after careful discussion with my family and prayerful consideration, I joined the United States Army Reserves and The Ohio Army National Guard. The reasons for joining the military were twofold which included the monthly financial assistance to assist with expenses and following the footsteps of other family members who have served in the military. Members of my family who have served in the military included my stepfather John W. Dunkley Sr. who served in the United States Army, my stepbrother John W. Dunkley Jr. who served in the United States Air Force and my favorite first cousin Command Sergeant Major Robert Ferris who had a distinguished career of serving 37 years in the United States Army. Incidentally, my brother Jerry would serve 20 years in the United States Navy and my younger brother Arthur would serve 4 years in the Army and 4 years in The Ohio Army National Guard. The exciting thing about joining the military was being part of a larger organization committed to serving our state and our country in times of need in addition to the educational opportunities of training at some of the best medical facilities in our country. When I was a sophomore medical student, I completed an active duty obstetrics and gynecology rotation at Brook Army Medical Center at Fort Sam Houston, San Antonio, Texas. This was a wonderful rotation for several reasons. The first reason was I able to deliver my first baby and the second reason was the experience of training in an active duty military hospital. More about my military experiences to come.

1983 was a busy year with medical school, joining the reserves in the National Guard as well as getting married in June 1983. I married Sharon Williams from Akron Ohio whom I met in my college Spanish class at the University of Akron. I also found out that she also worked at Akron City Hospital and had family members who were who worked in the medical field. Her mother was the afternoon charge nurse and her uncle, Dr.

Hayes H. Davis was a nephrologist there as well. Sharon had a baby son Terrell Williams.

Now I had a daughter Kristen, a wife Sharon and a stepson Terrell. The fact of having a family created additional stress while in medical school. Sharon had previously worked as a unit secretary at Akron City Hospital and unfortunately was unable to find a similar position in Athens Ohio. Most opportunities she investigated did not have a competitive salary. Therefore we made the decision that she would stay in Akron and work at Akron City Hospital. My daughter Kristen stayed in Akron with her mother Kathy. I was in Athens alone and was able to concentrate on my classes in medical school. I would regularly drive home to see Sharon, Terrell and Kristen. I was not the only student attending medical school from the Akron area. One of my best friends, David Cola was also from the Akron area and his wife Lynn was a graduate of Northeastern Ohio Universities College of Medicine (now NEOMED) and was an Obstetrician Gynecologist. Dave and I would travel to Akron on a regular basis to see our families.

The first 2 years of medical school went very fast and before I knew it we were preparing for our clinical years 3 and 4. There were various hospitals that were affiliated with our medical school and we had to use a lottery to determine where the students would go for their clinical rotations. I wanted a larger hospital and fortunately I got my first choice. I was selected to complete my clinical years at Drs. Hospital North and West in

Columbus, Ohio. Dr.'s Hospital North was in the short north area near downtown Columbus. Dr. West was on Broad Street on the west side of Columbus. Both hospitals were very busy and each had their respective surgical, orthopedic and internal medicine groups. I worked extremely hard on my clinical rotations which included general surgery, orthopedics, internal medicine, cardiology and emergency medicine. These rotations provided training and experiences in the core services that are beneficial to physicians in training.

My previous work experience and training in surgery provided comfort while being in a new hospital. Understanding how to interview and examine patients and more importantly how to conduct myself in the operating room seemed easy to me. This was all based on my previous experience and training with Dr. Forshew and other surgeons in the operating room at Akron City Hospital. By the time I reached my clinical sites for the third and fourth years, I decided I wanted to pursue orthopedic surgery as a career choice. I also found out that Drs. Hospital had a residency program and it was rumored the decision was made of whom they chose for the residency in 1986. Because of this rumor I made the decision to come back to Akron, Ohio where I thought I had a better chance of being more competitive for the residency slot at Cuyahoga Falls General Hospital. I interviewed and was accepted as an intern at Cuyahoga Falls General Hospital for the class entering 1986. There was also exciting news I was going to be a father again and ultimately my son

Gregory Brandon Hill was born on August 5, 1986. Once again I was stressed about being a dad, physician and husband and dedicating the appropriate time to each. Today we call this **work-life balance**. During my internship and residency I wasn't sure there was such a thing called *work-life balance*.

Internship

In the 1980s all osteopathic internships were considered rotating which meant the interns rotated on several different clinical rotations which included obstetrics and gynecology, general surgery, emergency medicine, orthopedics, intensive care and internal medicine. The majority of my energy was focused on my internship and then applying for a residency in orthopedics. Fortunately, I was selected as the top candidate to become a resident in the orthopedic surgery program at the hospital. In our internship and residency program I was one of two African-American residents at the hospital. Dr. Gregory Moton was the other African-American resident in the family practice residency at Cuyahoga Falls General. Following graduation from the residency program Dr. Moton practiced at our hospital for a number of years before leaving to pursue other opportunities.

I was very driven as an orthopedic resident and felt I needed to outperform the other residents in our program. Since high school I have always considered myself an overachiever. Remember, my mother told me many years ago that black professionals had to work harder and longer than their white counterparts to become successful. There were very few African-Americans who lived in Cuyahoga Falls during the 1980s. I was approached by a journalist from our local newspaper, the Akron Beacon Journal, who wanted to write a story on my experience as an African-American physician at Cuyahoga Falls General Hospital. We were both members of The New Hope Baptist Church. She wanted to interview me because I was 1 of a limited number of African-American interns at Cuyahoga Falls General Hospital. She specifically questioned me about my treatment at the hospital and whether I had encountered overt or covert discrimination from the staff or physicians at the hospital. This was further from the truth. I worked very hard during my internship and was well respected as a physician there. The article entitled *"Local Intern With Lofty Goals: Wants to Become Orthopedic Surgeon"* was ultimately published in the Akron Beacon Journal. However, there was an isolated incident while I was an intern that might be considered by some in the African-American community to be *"reverse discrimination"*. This means that the discrimination did not come from Non-African-Americans or Caucasians but the discrimination came from an African-American. Specifically, I was an intern in the OB service and was asked to examine a pregnant African-American female.

I introduced myself to the patient, explaining why I was there and that I needed to check her regarding the progress of her labor. She later reported to the nurses and my supervising physician she did not feel comfortable with me as her physician. I was immediately insulted, embarrassed with hurt feelings that an African-American patient would say those negative things about me. For those of you who are unfamiliar with the term *reverse discrimination*, this is a term that often emanated from the South when African-American patients did not feel comfortable with African-American physicians taking care of their medical needs because they felt that African-American physicians were inferior and not adequately trained. I shared this information with my attending physician who actually thought the whole thing was funny. This was the only time in my internship that I was insulted and embarrassed when an African-American patient expressed these emotions towards me.

Orthopedic Residency

Following my rotating internship I began my residency in 1987. At Cuyahoga Falls Hospital we had 3 attending physicians at our home hospital. Most of our faculty members were general orthopedic surgeons. Our residency was founded by Richard A. Josof, D.O. who also served as chairman of the orthopedic surgery department and residency program director. The other attending physicians were Howard A. Pinsky, D.O. and Paul J Deppisch, D.O. I was so excited to be chosen for the residency because I was one step closer to meeting my goal of becoming a surgeon. We had 5 residents at the time when I began the residency program. There was a progressive level of clinical responsibility which meant that at year one you learned how to take of patients on the floor and in the emergency room. In the second through the fifth years the residents learned how to perform surgeries under the direction of the attending surgeons. During our residency we were exposed to various sub-specialties of orthopedics which included trauma, sports medicine, pediatrics, pathology and hand surgery. The purpose of the various rotations was to have a comprehensive surgical experience representative of private practice.

During the fourth year of my orthopedic residency it was a requirement to obtain 3 months of pediatric orthopedic training in Cincinnati, Ohio at The Children's Hospital Medical Center of Cincinnati. I rotated with Alvin H. Crawford, MD, who was an esteemed pediatric orthopedic surgeon who had many years of experience as a pediatric surgeon, educator, and author as well as military experience in the Navy Reserves. Dr. Crawford was a tough taskmaster and conducted his service similar to that of a military unit with a commander, executive officer or XO and "*point man*". The point man was the resident who was assigned to Dr. Crawford's service and was responsible for organizing the journal club, knowing the condition of all of the pediatric orthopedics patients on the service and disseminating information to the rest of the residents on the service. Dr. Crawford always expected the residents to be prepared and to perform at a very high level. One of the things that he emphasized was to always respect the parents, be professional and honest with them. He would say if you do not know the answer say you do not know and look up the information and provide it to the patients as soon as possible. I was honored to train under Dr. Crawford and he ultimately became one of my mentors as well. Being tall, African-American, knowledgeable, and well-published were qualities that defined him. He had established a reputation among the pediatric orthopedic community and those who worked with him and for him.

Despite the fact the rotation was very stressful I considered it the best rotation I ever had as a resident. Probably the main reason the rotation was stressful was because Dr. Crawford had high expectations of the residents working with him. He often said "It is very painful to learn."

According to Dr. Crawford, a person has to acknowledge what they don't know and then proceed from there. Once a resident or student admits what they don't know, learning can occur. Dr. Crawford ignited a spark in me regarding giving back and becoming involved in the academic aspects of orthopedic training. I also felt as if mentoring was very important since someone reached out to me to show me the way to be a successful physician and leader.

Following my pediatric orthopedic rotation in Cincinnati Ohio I returned to Cuyahoga Falls General Hospital full of energy and motivation to teach our orthopedic residents in my newfound love of pediatric orthopedics. I was seriously considering a career in academics, working and teaching orthopedics at a medical school or an academic Medical Center. My conflict was being a divorced parent leaving my children in Akron and not being able to see them regularly.

In your own life, there will always be conflicts such as this. It may not look exactly like mine but there will be conflicts and you will often feel as if your work conflicts with your personal life. Work-life balance is something that has been written about since the beginning of time as a man searches for meaning and tries to find ways to have it all. Unfortunately, there may not be a way to have it all without a little bit of sacrifice in one way or another. All of this requires deep introspection. What season are you in? Will your family support you and understand if you have to choose a path that takes you away for a bit? Is that worth it to you? If this was your last month on earth would you make a different choice? If you only had limited time to spend with your loved ones would you choose that job over spending time with them? These are all of the decisions that every human has to make during his or her lifetime.

Post Residency Fellowship in Hand Surgery

Prior to graduation from my residency in 1991 my former wife and I separated and ultimately divorced in 1993. As you can imagine divorce while in a training program can be emotionally devastating. Regardless, one must remain emotionally balanced while taking care of patients as well as yourself. It is imperative for you to find balance for your mental health.

Following graduation from our residency program I was accepted to pursue a postgraduate Fellowship in Hand and Microsurgical Fellowship at the State University in New York at Buffalo. I had mixed emotions about the fellowship because I was in the process of divorce as well as starting a new training opportunity. There were two other fellows that year who were also responsible for covering the hand service at 4 hospitals. During our fellowship we treated complex cases from the surrounding communities in Buffalo, New York. The winters in Buffalo were extreme in terms of the amount of snow they received. Because of this, we became proficient in taking care of simple and complex snow blower injuries. In addition, we worked at Erie County Medical Center, a level 1 trauma center, and managed all aspects of hand and upper extremity musculoskeletal trauma. The trauma included injuries requiring microvascular reconstruction, treatment of simple and complex upper extremities fractures and congenital hand deformities at The Children's Hospital of Buffalo. In addition, it was not uncommon to treat patients with injuries sustained from gunshots and motor vehicle accidents.

Our fellowship practice was called "The Hand Center of Western New York" which was housed at Millard Fillmore Hospital. The hand center is a large orthopedic practice specializing in hand and upper extremity surgery consisting of 4 hand surgeons, 3 fellows, residents from the University of Buffalo orthopedic program and a large number of occupational hand therapists and support staff. I had a fantastic educational experience and had a sufficient amount of material to prepare us for both academic and clinical practices in orthopedics and hand surgery. Later, during my first year in practice I returned to Buffalo, New York for additional post-graduate training in Pediatric Orthopedics because of the hospital By-Law issues at some of the local hospitals in Akron. Once I completed the additional 3 months of training at The Buffalo Children's Hospital, I returned to Akron to resume full-time practice.

NOTES

CHAPTER FOUR
A NEW BEGINNING

Seasons are influenced by each change in your life. You're left to ponder which fork in the road you should take, overwhelmed by ideas, opportunities, your own heart, and sometimes even indecisiveness.

I had plans on returning to Akron to join North Hill Orthopedic Surgery Group which was the primary group responsible for our orthopedic residency training program. I was so honored to join the practice because they had offered me a position to join a group as a second-year resident. I was so excited about this new opportunity to become a practicing physician with a six-figure salary. This was more money than I had ever made. It was also more money than my parents had ever made. My divorce was final in 1993 and the court order set down the amount of alimony and spousal support I was ordered to pay. The amount of money paid seemed unreasonable to me but I believe this is the common thought by most men who go through this process. What led to the divorce?

Each side of any break up has its twist on things, but in my attempt to excel as a resident and cover our expenses I was away from home more and more. This proved to be detrimental to my marriage. I take the blame for that, and for my drive to succeed. Regardless of what happened with our relationship neither one of us wanted to see our children suffer. We both loved them first. Divorce is one of the most stressful things one can encounter and I would not recommend it to anyone. Emotional anxiety, ups and downs, and scheduling challenges arise when visiting with the ex-spouse.

Once I started private practice I decided to rent a house in Cuyahoga Falls, Ohio, since I wasn't sure where I wanted to live permanently. Private practice responsibilities, finding the optimal advantage to being a good dad, and maintaining good mental health all proved to be energy consuming.

North Hill Orthopedic Surgery Group consisted of 3 physicians, including the founder of the practice Richard A. Josof, D.O., Howard A Pinsky, D.O., and Paul Deppisch, D.O. This was an extremely exciting time for me. It was a great honor for me to be chosen to join their practice as a second-year resident. I thought this was pretty special.

Later, I learned how committing to a job opportunity very early often takes away your flexibility of being open minded and looking at other employment opportunities. My dream was finally realized-- I was a full-fledged fellowship trained orthopedic surgeon and I was fully prepared to start private practice. Starting the practice was very slow which is typical but I did participate in the call schedule which allowed me to develop a clientele of patients. After completing a fellowship in hand and upper extremity surgery, I was interested in the academic or teaching aspect of orthopedic surgery as well.

I began taking more responsibility and leadership in the fracture conference and the residency program. At one point during the early portion of my career in the mid to late 90s I considered pursuing an academic job opportunity at Ohio University Heritage College of Osteopathic Medicine. I interviewed at Ohio University with the Dean of the Medical School at that time, Dr. Barbara Ross Lee and began to give this new job opportunity serious consideration. Something was unsettling about the opportunity. I believe it really was not the opportunity of going to Athens to teach and practice orthopedic surgery but more importantly it had to do with me leaving my children in Akron and being away from them consistently. I was not comfortable being 3 hours away and visiting them on the weekends. After serious thought and consideration of the effect of leaving Akron would have on my children, I decided not to pursue the job opportunity. I explained my decision to Dr. Barbara Ross Lee about being an African-American dad not being present and the long-term effects it would have on them. Dr. Ross Lee responded and stated "I do not like your answer but I respect your answer." She also stated "At some point your children will grow up and if you still want to pursue an academic career in medicine those opportunities will be forever present."

She also stated that the students in medical school need to see someone who looks like you and you need to share your story with them. I often wonder what type of career I would have had in a full-time academic environment. Because of my interest in education, I became the assistant program director in 1996 and in 1999, I was appointed Program Director of the Orthopedic Residency Program at Cuyahoga Falls General Hospital.

Besides practicing orthopedic surgery, my children became my focal point and I was more interested in becoming a great dad to them compared to becoming an academic physician. At times, some of our weekends were challenging and complicated by my orthopedic call schedules. But when I looked back at this we actually had wonderful times together. It was an opportunity to be together regardless of what we were doing. When I had emergency surgery(s) on weekends, I would often take them to the hospital with me.

On the way to the hospital we would stop at McDonald's to pick up food for 3 children and of course me as well. We would take the food to the surgeons' lounge and the kids would eat breakfast and watch TV while I performed emergency surgery. My kids thought this was fun being in the hospital, interacting with the nurses and other doctors. At times they were able to watch me perform surgery through a viewing window. They followed me on rounds and would often sit at the nurses' station while I made rounds on my patients. Our time together was really wonderful. We spent time going to movies, parks, rollerblading as well as traveling. One of my fondest strips was traveling to Chicago and visiting the new Nike store as well as visiting basketball icon Michael Jordan's restaurant. The Nike store had all of the latest and greatest Tiger Woods golf shirts, and Michael Jordan basketball jerseys and workout clothes. I'm sure I spent too much money on many occasions but that's what parents love to do and it was a very enjoyable experience for me and my children.

Introduction to Administration and 9/11

As my clinical practice became busier I also took on more committee assignments and administrative duties at our hospital. In 2000 I became the Medical Staff president of Cuyahoga Falls General Hospital. The interesting thing was that I was responsible for the administrative policies and the clinical responsibilities of my orthopedic practice. My responsibility was to represent the medical staff regarding credentialing, policies and procedures and presiding over the Medical Executive Committee meetings. In 2001 due to financial hardships our hospital merged with a Summa Health System which was a level 1 trauma center in Akron.

However, as our merger began to take place there were often regularly scheduled meetings to familiarize both institutions with medical staff leadership, policies and procedures, and the plan going forward for this new relationship. Tom Strauss, CEO of Summa Health Systems asked me to stay an additional year as president of the medical staff at Cuyahoga Falls General Hospital. He stated I was very comfortable with the policies and procedures, rules and regulations and my presence would make the transition much easier for both institutions.

In 2000, I began dating the woman who would eventually become my wife. I met Judi Carol Bevly at the Arlington Church of God in Akron. When we met we both were dating other people and not ready to pursue a relationship. Judi was a teacher at Akron Public Schools with one daughter, Ariss. Finally, we both became available and introduced our teenage children to one another. Our kids seemed to get along and my daughter in particular asked if I was going to marry Judi? She went on to say, "Granny and I like her, we think she is the one for you." Well, here I go again with making a major decision and thinking about the pressure of settling down. I knew she was the one and so did other people who knew us both. One evening we went to a local restaurant for dinner, The Wine Merchant, in Merriman Valley. We saw a mutual friend there who commented, "Doc this is the one for you." Somehow I knew he was right.

We married on August 11, 2001 at our home church and included our children in a special ceremony where they exchanged vows to each other as siblings.

We married one month to *September 11, 2001* when our country was brutally attacked when the World Trade Center in New York City was hit by 2 hijacked airplanes. In addition, high jacked airplanes hit the Pentagon in D.C and an additional plane scheduled to hit the White House was diverted and crashed in rural Pennsylvania. Our country was stunned and many of our airports immediately shut down. Schools went on lockdown and children were sent home early. President George Bush was in Georgia reading to some elementary children when the attacks occurred. Once he returned to Washington D.C. he made an announcement that we would work to find the individuals responsible for 9/11 and take them out. Unfortunately, thousands of Americans were killed in the World Trade Center attack as well as losing soldiers and civilians in the Pentagon and passengers and crew on Flight 93 in rural Pennsylvania.

Immediately following this incident our Armed Forces went into action and overseas deployments occurred readily. President Bush had strong intelligence the bombing was the work of Osama Bin Laden from Afghanistan. As more and more troops were deployed, I became nervous and concerned that I would eventually be activated for the war.

I had been in the Army Reserves for almost 20 years and had never been activated for a combat war deployment. We were contacted by our National Guard unit and were told more than likely we would be deployed but they cannot give us any detail as to when that would occur. As a reservist, our unit, Ohio

Medical Detachment Company of the Ohio Army National Guard would meet monthly for our regular weekend drills. After 9/11 we would perform Pre-mobilization Physical Exams on members of the Ohio Army National Guard and the Air National Guard. This was to examine the soldiers' units who were preparing for deployment to Afghanistan and later Iraq. Once 9/11 occurred our mission and responsibilities to our home unit changed. We became more focused on our training because many of us would eventually be deployed to combat. On occasion some soldiers were disqualified from deployment for a myriad of reasons. Some of these included medical conditions such as heart problems, orthopedic issues, uncontrolled diabetes and kidney problems.

One interesting note is with all of the excitement of the war in Afghanistan there were rumors and concerns from Washington about there being a war starting in Iraq. The discussion centered on the topic of weapons of mass destruction and whether Saddam Hussein was involved in the 9/11 attack. The other claim was Saddam Hussein was responsible for killing and assassinating the residents of Iraq. Unfortunately, there was mixed intelligence regarding the truth of this information. General Colin Powell disclosed to Congress and our nation that there was evidence of weapons of mass destruction. Credible evidence of "Weapons of Mass Destruction" would help Congress convince the American public of the importance of sending additional troops to a war in Iraq. General Colin Powell was a retired 4-star general who also served as Secretary of State and the Chairman of the Joint Chiefs of Staff. Gen. Powell was generally well respected by those in government as well as the American people.

General Powell's presentation was well received and Congress ultimately voted to send troops to Iraq. Regretfully, we later learned some of the intelligence given to General Powell was inaccurate. We were now involved in two wars being fought at the same time. One in Afghanistan and the other in Iraq. The majority of our communities agreed to aid the United States in our efforts to safeguard our homeland from further acts of terrorism. It was strange and exciting at the same time to see so many young people wanting to enlist in the military and do their part to defend and protect our country.

I regularly received information from my unit regarding the possibility of being deployed. This information was shared with my orthopedic partners regarding the probability of being deployed to support the military efforts in either Afghanistan or Iraq. As both wars progressed and we lost more troops I became more nervous about when my time would come for deployment. Spending time with my family became the most important thing to me. My brother Jerry was an active duty Navy and his unit was already deployed to the Middle East to support Operation Iraqi Freedom. The probability of having a second son deployed in the war weighed heavy on my mother. She was a woman of faith but this stress was very noticeable on her mental health and wellbeing, and the day did indeed finally arrive.

The Call to Serve

The call finally came on a Thursday afternoon following a full day of surgery at Cuyahoga Falls General Hospital. I was sitting in the recovery room finishing post-operative orders when the call came. I was told there was a phone call for me and I asked who was calling. I was told it was Colonel Donald Ulrich, our commander of the medical attachment unit of the Ohio Army National Guard. As you can imagine, I immediately became anxious before answering the phone. I picked up the phone and responded, "Colonel how can I help you, Sir?"

He had general questions about my well-being and how things were going with my practice. He quickly got to the point of the phone call when he commented: "The orthopedic surgeons in Iraq are getting hammered and we need some additional support from our orthopedic surgeons." I quickly responded, "What does that have to do with me, sir?" He told me, "I need you to volunteer to support the troops and the doctors in Iraq."

I immediately began to feel uncomfortable regarding his request, and I began to stammer and make excuses about why I was not suitable for deployment. My comments included, "I'm newly married and probably this is not the best option for me at this time."

In addition, I commented that my practice was busy and I was not sure that my partners would support the idea of me being deployed (of course they didn't get a vote). Then I began to feel uncomfortable about the multitude of excuses I was making about honoring the call to serve.

My mind went back to my values, as I listened on the phone.

I joined the military on March 10, 1983 during my first year of medical school and was introduced to the Army Core Values at that time. These values are important in my life and serve as a template of how I live my life and how I treat people. I began to think about the 7 Core Army Values soldiers are supposed to live by which include **Loyalty, Duty, Integrity, Respect, Selfless Service, Honor** and **Personal Courage**. I was reminded of the military oath of office. This is an oath of office for both officers and enlisted service members to support and defend the Constitution of the United States of America. Once service members commit to the United States Armed Forces, the oath of office is cited as part of the in-taking process before basic training takes place.

It reads: *"I Gregory Hill, do solemnly swear or affirm that I will support and defend the Constitution of the United States against all enemies, foreign or domestic; that I will bear true faith and allegiance to the same; that I take this obligation freely, without any mental reservation or purpose of evasion; and that*

I will well and faithfully discharge the duties of the office on which I am about to enter. So help me God."

After thinking of the oath of office and the Army Core Values, I responded to Colonel Ulrich, "If I am put on orders sir I would be honored to serve."

He reassured me with these words, "Very good and I will make sure your orders are cut or released within 3 weeks." We exchanged polite remarks and he thanked me for my commitment and service. Of course after this less than 10-minute phone call I had a multitude of feelings including the fear of dying in combat, the stress of the unknown being in a combat zone deployment and not having been in an active war before. Additional stresses included wondering what my wife would think and how she would feel as well as my mother's feelings about it all. What do I say to my children and what would they think about their father going to war and facing the possibility of death?

My first phone call was to my wife Judi and I explained to her with anxiety and sadness that the long awaited phone call had finally come and I would be placed on orders to be deployed in support of Operation Iraqi Freedom. As Colonel Ulrich suggested my active duty orders arrived in 3 weeks. My orders revealed I would go on active duty approximately 1 week before Thanksgiving in November 2003. It also revealed my point of pre-mobilization training would take place at Fort Bliss Army Base in El Paso,

Texas. Fort Bliss was chosen as a training site because it resembled the weather pattern of the desert of the Middle East. The nights are extremely chilly and the days are very hot often close to 100 degrees. I was told this was a great place to train to become acclimated to the desert of Iraq. The next 2 months flew by as I prepared for deployment and mobilization.

The pre-mobilization checklist is very exhausting. Any soldier being deployed to a combat zone must have the following items in place: an up-to-date medical record file, will, updated life insurance policy and a power of attorney.

This entire process was extremely stressful on Judi and after I mentioned I was being deployed to my mother she commented, "Why are they sending you to war? You're too old to go to war!"

I told my mother that as a soldier I had taken the oath and it was my time and responsibility to serve. After careful thought, prayer and deliberation she later said she believed "The Lord would certainly put His arms around you to protect you while you're gone."

Of course this is another situation where my faith was surely tested. The fear of the unknown, going into combat, and facing the possibility of death or significant injury with resultant dismemberment was extremely stressful as you can imagine. However, I truly thought my faith was strong enough to sustain me through any deployment.

In addition to notifying my family, I had to notify my partners at North Hill Orthopedic Surgery group as well as friends and coworkers, fraternity brothers and my church family. One of my partners who had never served in the military had questions about why I was still in the reserves and whether my impetus for serving was the monetary aspect of serving. I came to find out he was only concerned about how this would affect his overhead or his share of the expenses. Having a full-fledged partner in the orthopedic group being sent to war was totally new for all of us. I had to protect myself and the group while I was deployed. Therefore, we added an amendment to my contract that allowed my overhead to be reduced by 50% and that any additional revenues would be passed on to my wife while I was deployed. We also agreed no major changes in our group would occur before I returned following my 90-day deployment. That proved not to be the case as I found out leadership changes were made while I was deployed on active duty. This was upsetting to me because it seemed that we did not follow the policies that we enacted during my discussion before I left for active duty. As part of planning for my deployment, we reviewed my financials and determined that I was able to take my bonus. These funds were given to my wife to cover expenses while I was away.

The closer I was to deployment the more nervous I became. I think it was the fear of the unknown of being in a combat zone and the realization of confronting major injuries and the possibility of death.

There were several employees in our hospital who either had sons or daughters who were in the reserves or active duty that were tapped for active duty to support either Operation Iraqi Freedom or Operation Enduring Freedom. Operation Iraqi Freedom supported troops in the mission against Iraq and Operation Enduring Freedom supported the mission in Afghanistan. Celebrations were held at the hospital and my private practice to mark my departure while I was deployed. I had mixed emotions about the parties for deployment. While I enjoyed the parties on my behalf, I was deeply concerned and stressed about being deployed to an area of the world I had only read about in the Bible. I had no inkling of what was to come.

Deployment Number 1

I reviewed my deployment orders and was ready to leave for my pre-mobilization duty station at Fort Bliss Army Base in El Paso, Texas. The orders normally give you a designated time and place for your arrival. There are specific instructions for transportation, arrival designation and points of contact and phone numbers.

The day came and my wife, mother and children escorted me to the Cleveland Hopkins Airport. I checked in at the airport. Before departing for my gate, we had a prayer and said our goodbyes. The good thing was that I was able to contact my family on a regular basis while I was at Fort Bliss. So, I spoke to my wife before being 'shipped' out to Iraq. Once I arrived at Fort Bliss I checked in and went through the process to obtain housing, meal times and instructions to report for training as well as the generalized schedule for the first week. Of course, once I checked into my room I looked at the schedule and made sure I was available for the first meeting the following day.

I arrived at the orientation meeting which outlined the general plan for the next 14 days at Fort Bliss and what the training schedule would be like. We also received the instructions about the dos and don'ts of traveling on and off base and specifically no travel zones such as Juarez. We were informed Juarez is in Mexico and the U.S. Army had no jurisdiction on going to Mexico. Apparently, in the past there had been soldiers who visited Juarez for excitement only to never return to Fort Bliss. The pre-authorization training consisted of every facet that one can imagine. It involved daily physical fitness training which consisted of push-ups, sit-ups, and running. Additional training included more specific military training such as range fire, agility drills and explosive training. We picked up uniforms for deployment and any additional items necessary for the trip. As a physician I quickly found out who the other physicians and medical providers were. This was necessary for our training and we all needed to work together to accomplish our goals. The physical fitness portion of the training did not seem overly difficult because I worked out on a regular basis while I was at home. There were certain agility drills required such as climbing and crawling through the desert under wires with a weapon on our backs. As expected I would be deployed in a combat zone requiring a soldier to know how to use a weapon. Therefore, there was required range training either using an M16 or a 9 mm. An M16 is the standard weapon for an enlisted soldier. The 9 mm is the standard military issue handgun/weapon for an officer. Because of my rank at that time and being a Medical Corps officer the 9mm was my assigned weapon.

In the past while a regular reservist, we participated in range training while on active duty at Camp Grayling, Michigan. Previously, I received the honor of being a Marksman Shooter and once had a perfect score. So I thought I felt comfortable being on the shooting range including disarming, cleaning, and assembling and disassembling the weapon. However, I did not shoot on a regular basis except for summer camp in Michigan and certainly from my performance at Fort Bliss I was a bit rusty. The objective of this exercise was to shoot a pop-up target that was triggered by a time-release pop-up. Following the range exercise, I was informed that I did not pass. What a humbling experience!

I was embarrassed and surprised because I had previously been proficient in marksmanship and shooting. Technically because I did not pass the shooting exercise the first day-- I and other soldiers who failed were required to come back the following day to requalify using our weapons. I was actually embarrassed by the fact that I had been a soldier for a number of years and actually did not pass the firing test. However, I returned to the firing range the following day and had a discussion with the range officer before starting our qualification process. The range officer inquired about my handedness-- being left or right-handed. I responded that "I am right-handed." Following this he inquired which of my eyes were dominant. My response was "I am not sure." He gave me a simple exercise and stated that if I hold a triangle in front of my face with my right eye closed, where is the triangle? If the triangle is in the front of my face then I am left eye dominant. However, if I close my left-eye and the triangle is in the middle then I am right-eye dominant. Despite the fact that I had been in the reserves for so long I was never instructed on this technique to determine which eye was dominant. It appears at times I would close the right or the left eye and this probably was the reason why on any given day I had random scores. Once I determined I was left-eye dominant I quickly completed the range fire drill and progressed to the next section of pre-mobilization training.

Overall the pre-mobilization experience was not overwhelming. There were a number of routine things we had to do including agility drills, physical training (running and calisthenics, range fire and medical evaluation. In addition, we had to make sure our deployment immunizations were up-to-date. On the day of our immunizations we all had to arrive, stand in long lines and go through the process of receiving up to approximately 7 shots before we were eligible for deployment. Many of the soldiers unfortunately did not handle the immunizations very well. Some became lightheaded or fainted or complained of severe arm soreness in the days following the injections.

Also, after I arrived at Fort Bliss I found out the location of my final assignment. My orders included the instruction I would be assigned to the First Forward Surgical Team in support of the 28th Combat Support Hospital from Fort Bragg, North Carolina. The 28th Combat Support Hospital is an active duty hospital unit that was deployed in 1990 in the Gulf War and was the first hospital unit established and deployed in Iraq in support of Operation Iraqi Freedom. The professionalism, discipline, organization, and operational efficiency of this unit were top-notch. After receiving my orders for deployment to Baghdad, Iraq I quickly met other soldiers who were deployed to the same area. We became a close-knit unit with the same goals of supporting the mission which included providing support and care for the troops, being safe at all times and for the entire unit to return together. My best battle buddy was Colonel Michael Cruz who was a general surgeon from the island of Guam. We found out that we both loved San Diego, California because of the weather. I had family there and we both agreed we liked vacationing there. We joked about making a pact that we would retire and move to San Diego. One of the things that stuck with me was that we both agreed "Do not let me do anything stupid to prevent me from returning home to our families."

The 28th Combat Support Hospital was an active-duty hospital, with plenty of surgeons to care for soldiers. Colonel Cruz was a general surgeon but there was no room for an additional surgeon to work at the Hospital in Baghdad. Therefore his assignment changed and he was assigned to the headquarters in the Green Zone in Baghdad, Iraq. Col Cruz would still visit the hospital and regularly check in on me. He would share information about his new assignments that often took him into the city of Baghdad and surrounding communities. Many of his assignments were fairly dangerous but he remained safe and suffered no injuries. We were deployed to Baghdad together and redeployed (went home) simultaneously and vowed to stay in touch. I truly consider him a lifelong friend and battle buddy.

As a surgeon in America, you go through many battles with colleagues. You face highs and lows. But as a surgeon in combat, you face death and survival together. It was truly life-changing.

In November 2003, Thanksgiving arrived and Fort Bliss was closed due to the holiday. We had no required responsibilities, physical training (PT), range fire, or meetings. Thanksgiving is my favorite holiday because of the sense of family but it saddened me because I was not with my family back in Ohio. So, our newfound family at Fort Bliss and soldiers assigned to the First Forward Surgical team met at a family restaurant to have a buffet dinner.

We prepared for our overseas deployment a couple of days following Thanksgiving with the anticipated arrival in Baghdad, Iraq around November 28 or 29. We received instructions about our flight plans which included traveling from Fort Bliss to an active duty post in Georgia to pick up additional soldiers, followed by travel to Germany. We had about 100 soldiers being deployed to the Middle East which required an extremely large plane. The military had charted a flight that allowed us to bring all of our gear including weapons. Normally, on commercial airlines, civilian passengers cannot travel with firearms unless they have active duty orders and/or have a special permit to carry a loaded weapon. Otherwise the weapons must be secured and locked up.

This was an extremely large plane and we had plenty of room to move around. Considering the flight length, we were relatively comfortable and in good company since everyone on the plane was on active duty headed to Iraq.

Our total flight time from Texas to Baghdad, Iraq was approximately 28 hours. We stopped in Germany to refuel, have briefings, meet other soldiers and prepare for the trip to Kuwait. We were in Kuwait for approximately 24 to 30 hours depending on specific travel schedules and points of destination. As a reservist, our orders outlined what is termed 90 days boots on the ground. 90 days boots on the ground were structured for United States Army Reserve and Ohio Army National Guard physicians who had private practices back in the states. It had been determined that specific reserve military physicians could be away from their practice for approximately 90 days without suffering significant financial hardship. Once we arrived in Kuwait this actually started the clock for what was considered the first day of deployment in the country.

Regretfully, active duty physicians did not have the option of limited deployments or duty assignments. Normally active duty physicians assigned to a large unit are deployed to the unit and spend the entire time on deployment with that particular unit. Normally in combat, those active duty assignments were 12 to 13 months before the unit was returned home or redeployed. Reserve physicians may have their tour of duty extended at times due to extenuating circumstances like the need for additional physicians to support the mission. Our travel assignment from Kuwait to Baghdad was finalized. We were to deploy at night and arrive in Baghdad several hours after the departure. The flight from Kuwait to Baghdad was very interesting because we flew on a C17. The interesting thing about a C17 is that the seats are essentially turned backward compared to the normal configuration of a commercial plane.

We took off without any problems and as we got closer to Baghdad, Iraq we were told to prepare for combat landing. Immediately, I felt very uncomfortable by this because I had never heard of such a thing. So, I quickly turned to the individual sitting next to me and I said, "What the hell is a combat landing?" He responded, "That means lean forward and prepare for a crash landing." I thought oh my God there is nothing I can do to change this. Immediately, I felt stressed and anxious because I had no control and my fate was left to our pilot and God. We landed without any problems and I felt mixed emotions about finally being in Baghdad, Iraq. I was excited and nervous at the same time. I had a question for the soldier sitting next to me, "Why is it important to have us prepare for a combat landing?" His response was, "The Iraqi soldiers are always shooting at us upon arrival but fortunately for us they do not shoot straight!"

I thought, oh my goodness! Those soldiers who were traveling to Baghdad, Iraq gathered their gear and met with our transport team, who would be driving us to our new home. We noticed we were not traveling in a large vehicle or a truck but in a hospital ambulance. This really created a lot of anxiety but there was little I could do about it. We were also instructed, "We are now in a combat zone and it is necessary for you to have your weapons available, locked and loaded with the safety on." The purpose of this was to protect ourselves from enemy fire while we were going to the hospital. We were transported to our new home in the Green Zone without incident and I was relieved I was at my final destination. My commitment was to stay in Baghdad until I was redeployed back home in February 2004. I have arrived at my room assignment, introduced myself to my roommates, unpacked my bags, and arranged my new living arrangement for the next 90 days. My new roommate was an

GREGORY HILL, D.O.

active duty full bird colonel from Fort Sam Houston who was an oncologic gynecologist. Specifically, he dealt with female patients/soldiers who had gynecologic cancers. Considering our active duty environment we did not have any patients who needed his services.

The Bagdad Experience

At first the Baghdad experience was new and exciting because I was actually on an active duty post in a combat zone. I was assigned the responsibilities of being on the orthopedic call schedule following my introduction to the two existing orthopedic surgeons. They were deployed there since the U.S. had taken over Baghdad in March 2003. The military had a process of transitioning new surgeons to a particular work environment by setting up or establishing what is known as a "right seat/left seat."

The purpose of this was to bring in a new physician or surgeon and have him work side-by-side with the surgeon who will eventually be redeployed back home. This process allows the new surgeon to receive pertinent information about the dos and don'ts of deployment, and opportunities for best practices. This is done to ensure the new incoming surgeons are comfortable with the process of accepting phone calls, scheduling and performing surgeries and seeing patients in the emergency room.

One of the things that concerned me was taking orthopedic call in a combat zone. I was concerned because in my private practice back in Ohio I had a nice established practice that did not include level 1 trauma. However, in my residency I did have clinical training in level 1 trauma. The trauma we treat in combat zones is far more complex, complicated, and sophisticated than in the civilian world. Many of the injuries sustained in a combat zone consist of large and small arms fire as well as improvised explosive devices and burns.

An example of this occurred when I received a call about one of our soldiers who sustained a complex lower extremity injury. The soldier had been in a firefight and had received a gunshot wound to his lower leg. He sustained a complex open fracture of the tibia, and fibula as well as an open foot injury. These types of injuries can be devastating when bone is exposed, and there's tissue loss and 2 different levels of an injury. These types of injuries are also problematic if there is a vascular or blood supply issue. This was my first complicated open lower extremity injury. Fortunately, the senior orthopedic surgeon was on call with me and asked me if I wanted his assistance to begin the case. He was agreeable to assist me in the surgery. He responded, "I am sure you know how to do this but you cannot approach this like a hand surgeon."

He told me to follow the principles of treatment of an open injury and plan to apply an external fixator to stabilize the bone, clean the wound and minimize any chances of infection. An external fixator is a device consisting of large threaded pins, clamps, nuts and bolts and connection bars. Technically, the pins are placed into the bone using a drill and the pins are then connected by clamps and connection bars. The purpose of this is to stabilize the bone in a rigid manner to minimize excessive motion which can be very painful. The senior surgeon assisted me at the beginning of the procedure. He asked me where I wanted to place the first pin. I gave him specific landmarks and placed the pin in the appropriate position. He responded, "Correct" and following this he asked about the second pin placement which I correctly responded regarding the precise location. I followed his instruction and he briefly looked at me and said, "You are just fine. You got this and I am leaving." As he departed the room he said, "Remember you're now a trauma surgeon and do not treat these injuries like a hand surgeon." He pulled off his gown and gloves and left the room and finally I was on my own. I quickly became acclimated to the trauma environment in the Green Zone and felt like one of the members of the team.

The Green Zone was a fortified area in Iraq inhabited by American troops, government contractors and some Iraqi workers including translators. In addition, the Green Zone also housed our headquarters, which consisted of Finance, Operations and Supply. These sections are required for the operation and administration of an active duty base to manage and take care of our troops regarding finance, housing, meals and support.

In addition, there was a flea market in the Green Zone which provided access to purchase gifts, and trinkets for our rooms such as flash drives, cameras, blankets and souvenirs. I had never seen a flash drive until I arrived in Iraq. The flash drives were used to transfer audio and picture data files. It seemed everyone had a flash drive so I thought I had to have one as well. I later found out the flea market was not authorized for visitation by the American troops. Like other soldiers, I went to the flea market to buy items for my room. I always felt the flea market was unsafe because of a lack of security. This proved to be true later after I returned home and read there was an explosion at the flea market and some of our troops were severely injured.

We had a morning report which occurred daily at 7 AM to review the clinical activity or combat injuries from the previous night. We also received up-to-date information on hospital census, patient evacuation plans and intelligence regarding the movement of the enemy.

I established some great relationships during my stay and met some salt of the earth soldiers and leaders. Approximately one month into my rotation I was told there was a reserve medical unit from Ohio who would be joining us. I received information from my roommate that their commander was from Akron, Ohio as well. I figured I had to know this surgeon but I was told he had a funny name. My roommate said I believe he is a cardiothoracic surgeon and I asked if his name was Michael Oddi and he responded yes! He then mentioned he was right down the hall. I walked down to the room and knocked on the door. The door opened and we both were surprised to see each other. We hugged and shared a quick conversation about our deployment. I commented, "I had to travel over 6 thousand miles to see a guy from Akron, Ohio." Col. Oddi commented that his assignment was to build a prison hospital in the Anbar Province near Fallujah. Considering the area's history of frequent and fierce battles, the thought of constructing a prison hospital was a cause for concern. One of my most memorable cases occurred in early December 2003 when a Time Magazine reporter sustained a severe traumatic amputation of the right hand. Michael Weisskopf was covering a story in Iraq on the effects and the morale of the soldiers deployed there. While riding in a military vehicle through the streets in the green zone, a young man was running through the streets and he tossed a canister into the military vehicle. Unbeknownst to Michael Weiskopf he picked up the grenade canister to toss it out of the vehicle and then it exploded. He lost his right hand through the wrist joint and was transported to our Combat Trauma Facility, Ibn Sina Hospital in Baghdad, Iraq. I was on call the night he came in and I introduced myself "My name is Major Gregory Hill and I'm the orthopedic surgeon on call tonight and I'll be taking care of you." I began to examine him regarding the complexity of his injuries. Mr. Weisskopf quickly commented about being recently divorced and a custodial parent. His question was whether he would be able to drive his kids to school? I responded with confidence, "We have the technology to give you a functional extremity with a prosthesis."

Following our orthopedic triage we stabilized his injuries and prepared him for surgery. In surgery we amputated the damaged tissue and admitted him to our hospital. He had one additional surgery before he was evacuated to Germany. Mr. Weisskopf had additional surgeries in Germany and at Walter Reed Hospital in the United States. He would later contact me in Akron to discuss a book he was writing. I vividly remember the messages from the Army "There was someone from *Time Magazine* wanting to speak to you." I was asked if I remembered taking care of a Time Magazine journalist and I responded, "Absolutely I remembered taking care of a journalist." I was in the office of North Star Orthopedics when we finally connected. The phone call began with "Major Hill.... this is Michael Weisskopf ... I'm not sure you remember me" and I quickly responded, "YES, I know who you are!"

He further commented he was writing a book and wanted my permission to be included in the book. I was honored Mr. Weisskopf requested my permission to put my name in his book. Before my conversation ended, I became very emotional as our call took me back to the combat zone in Baghdad.

One of the other young soldiers in the vehicle with Mr. Weisskopf also sustained injuries to his back and knee. When I interacted with him, he identified as James Beverly. I asked further to know where Private Beverly calls home. He answered, "Akron, Ohio sir." And I said, "No way can you be from Akron." I later got to find out that he attended Green High School. Green High School is located in the southern portion of Summit County approximately 25 minutes from downtown Akron.

Following our brief interaction, I was able to make him feel more comfortable since his injuries were not as severe as others. He would later reach out to me once he was back in Akron, Ohio. There were other members of the team who were injured in the grenade attack but none sustained severe injuries like Mr. Weisskopf.

My first deployment progressed quickly. We were very busy with orthopedic injuries because of Improvised Explosive Devices (IEDs). These were man-made bombs that had nails, glass, rocks or anything that might cause damage. The Iraqis were very creative in making bombs. Cars were frequently utilized as storage and as the actual bomb. These were called Vehicle Born Improvised Explosive Devices (VBIDS). Explosives were often placed under the axle, radiator or in the trunk. The enemy would often use the car as the actual bomb. As you might imagine these bombs killed thousands of our soldiers and caused devastating injuries to many more. Many of the bombs caused complex extremity injuries because of our leaded vests. There were leaded extremity coverings available but many soldiers complained the additional weight slowed them down while on maneuvers because it made traveling challenging.

During combat we are faced with stress upon stress when we encounter battlefront injuries or lose members of our unit. In my opinion, working closely with fellow soldiers has created lifelong relationships. There is a special bond or brotherhood we experience. Perhaps you've heard *"The Band of Brothers."* It really is true. During the quiet times we read books, wrote in our journals or watched movies to pass the time away. To keep things halfway normal we always celebrated birthdays when given the opportunity. One thing we quickly learned was there was no alcohol on base.

It seemed the time flew by and before I knew it my 90 days were almost up. We were notified that we would be receiving a new orthopedic surgeon. The surgeon arrived and we noted he was a hand surgeon from Texas. After brief a conversation, I found out that I actually knew his partner who is originally from Youngstown Ohio. His name was Paul Phillips III and we often worked closely together on complex upper extremity cases since our backgrounds were very similar. The time came for me to prepare for redeployment back home. However, in talking to the Air Force which was responsible for transport home I found out I could be a patient transporter and fly to Germany. This increased my chances of getting home without delay. So, I became a patient escort and flew to Landstuhl, Germany for my patient drop off. My battle buddy, Colonel Michael Cruz also flew to Germany as a patient escort. I had the opportunity to visit Landstuhl Regional Medical Center which is a larger trauma center. We arrived in Germany without any problem and essentially stayed there for approximately 24 hours before we took our flight back to Fort Bliss in El Paso, Texas. It was necessary to return to our pre-mobilization site to return gear, and your weapon and take an exit physical examination including a mental health assessment. The military wanted to make sure soldiers were fit to return home without significant war issues such as post-traumatic stress disorder (PTSD). Soldiers returning to Fort Bliss were there anywhere from 3 to 7 days before orders were processed for redeployment home. I'll comment about PTSD in a later chapter.

Due to security issues in Iraq we were not allowed to tell our family members when we were leaving the combat zone. At times our families didn't know where we were at any given moment. Once we were in Kuwait, Germany or the Continental United States (CONUS) we could call our loved ones.

The Journey Home

As you can imagine, I was excited about returning home to my family. When I arrived at Cleveland Hopkins Airport, my family was there to meet me. My wife, mother, children and siblings were all there to celebrate my safe return home. We had a wonderful celebration once I returned to Copley. I felt and looked great and was proud of the work I had done overseas. I had lost about 10 pounds and was in great shape. I still had some additional time off before I returned to work. Leaving my battle buddies too soon was a strange feeling I experienced and I felt a sense of unfinished work.

Although I was happy to be home, I was not happy to return to my practice. While in Iraq there were decisions made regarding our practice I was concerned about. I felt we did not follow some of our policies and this was bothersome to me. Hence, I became restless about staying with the group long term. I entertained the idea of looking at other practice opportunities but I was more concerned about being deployed again.

My Second Deployment

My practice at North Star Orthopedics quickly returned to its pre-deployment level in terms of patient volume and number of surgeries scheduled. However, I was concerned about the unknown of future deployments as well as my practice situation. When I returned from my first deployment, I began having a conversation with a friend and former resident Wade Faerber, D.O. He was the program director of the orthopedic residency at Riverside Regional Medical Center in Moreno Valley, California. He stated they needed another hand surgeon for their group. I began to think about making the move to California but my mistake was not discussing this opportunity in more detail with my wife Judi and my kids. Judi and I were invited to California for an interview but according to Judi it all seemed so fast. We met with the partners and visited the office and the county hospital. They wined and dined us and made the opportunity look exciting. However, my wife was not excited about moving because leaving Akron at that time would significantly affect her retirement from Akron Public Schools. Finally, after a lengthy discussion we decided I would go to California and get established and she would move there later. We flew out there to look at apartments in Temecula about 71 miles north of San Diego. We both thought the good thing about Temecula was it was close to San Diego where Judi's sister, Lena and her brother-in-law Dale live. San Diego has always been one of our favorite cities in the U.S.

While we were entertaining the decision to move to southern California, I was contacted by our headquarters in Columbus, Ohio. I was needed for a second deployment. Initially, my orders reflected I was to be activated in January 2005 but I was able to delay the deployment until August 2005. The time from March until August 2005 flew by and I had to make a final decision about staying with my group. August arrived and I left for Fort Bliss in El Paso, Texas. The process of the second pre-mobilization was much easier than the second time. Once again we went through the check-in process, obtaining our lodging assignment and our overall schedule for our 2 weeks of training. I was looking forward to going back to Baghdad only to find out I had a new assignment. I was assigned to the 55th Brigade Combat Team from Louisiana.

The unit was assigned to a region in Iraq called the Anbar Province. This region was highly volatile and significant battles were fought there. Combat casualties were plentiful in Fallujah, Iraq. I was stationed in Kuwait for only a few days before arriving in Fallujah. Fortunately, I arrived without any issues and was under the impression I would be transported by helicopter only to find out in the morning there was no helicopter and I would be picked up by ground transport. The next morning arrived and I met the new unit soldiers, the transport team, and the travel commander. We went through the travel plans and I received my assignment. By that I meant while riding to our new base I was given the assignment of protecting the right back part of the vehicle and personnel with my nine millimeter weapon.

The ride to Camp Hit (Pronounced Heat) was stressful for several reasons:

- I was in unfamiliar territory or geography in the desert without significant backup (additional troops with larger weapons).
- I wasn't sure how long the trip would take through the desert to arrive at our camp.
- I had never been in an active duty convoy subject to being ambushed.
- I was concerned about roadside bombs. Speaking of roadside bombs, we did have to stop during our trip because our driver suspected a bomb was near and radioed in for the military robot to come and evaluate the situation. We waited for the robot which came in about 30 minutes. The robot completed the inspection and the next thing we heard was a loud boom! I thought

oh my goodness it was a bomb! The convoy resumed and we arrived at Camp Hit without any casualties. Camp Hit was located between Haditha and Ramadi in Northwest Iraq.

We completed our check-in, obtained lodging, met our commander, and the rest of the medical staff. I was unimpressed by my lodging, not by the size of the room or my roommates but by the fact that our room door did not lock. In my mind this created a significant security issue because we were at risk of unannounced individuals entering our room at night. So, I felt it was necessary to at least protect myself and sleep with my 9mm weapon under my pillow. When I was on call at night, I required my staff to knock before entering our room so I wasn't startled. It took some time to become used to sleeping in a room with an unlocked door. Once again my faith was tested traveling through the desert to Camp Hit and sleeping in an unlocked room for almost 3 months during my deployment.

After I settled in I began to ask questions about the history of Camp Hit and what unit was there before we arrived. We were told there was a Marine Unit that suffered significant casualties from a camp ambush and improvised explosive devices. I quickly recalled it was the 25th Marine Regiment, 3rd Battalion, 4th Marine Division from Brook Park, Ohio. The unit lost 14 marines in one attack and 7 marines in a separate attack. I had actually attended the memorial service which was held at the IX Center because so much of the community was affected.

This created a strange feeling because I felt as though I was spiritually close to the individuals who were from Ohio. Camp Hit was considered a Forward Operating Base or a FOB. We're often asked questions about what is a FOB and where are they in relationship to the battlefield? If the soldier is injured on the battlefield and needs first aid care by his battle buddy that is considered level 1 or buddy aid. Level 2 is the Forward Operating Base which is the next level of care after a buddy has stabilized an injured Marine or soldier. The care involved at a Forward Operating Base is essentially triage and stabilization, bandaging suturing, splinting of fractures, and preparation for evacuation to a level 3 or a Combat Support Hospital (CSH). The care at a Combat Support Hospital involves stabilization of severe traumas with extensive injuries, burns and care of patients needing intensive care. For example, my first deployment involved being assigned to the 1st Forward Surgical Team which was embedded in the 28th Combat Support Hospital in Baghdad, Iraq. We performed surgeries on patients who sustained complex trauma injuries that included fractures, large and small caliber gunshot wounds, burns, and neurosurgical injuries from explosions during our time in Baghdad. The medical care at a Forward Operating Base is to stabilize and triage to the next level of care or return to duty. There is no time or personnel for long drawn-out procedures.

Once these patients were stable enough to travel they were shipped to a level III trauma hospital in Baghdad or a level IV facility in Landstuhl Regional Medical Center in Germany. At Landstuhl Regional Army Medical Center they handle many more complex and sophisticated injuries. Patients can receive more detailed and definitive care due to the fact that it is not in a combat zone.

I quickly acclimated to the routine at Camp Hit. The typical day consisted of early rise, in line for the trailer shower (Portable Shower) followed by the chow. We weren't a large unit so we didn't have a formal kitchen like the one in Baghdad. We had processed eggs, ultra-processed milk, fruit and oatmeal. Needless to say, I lost weight while on the second deployment as well as the first. We didn't have normal clinic hours because we were a FOB. We were only busy when there was combat activity outside the wire (refers to activity near direct combat areas). We had time for working out and opportunities to teach the younger soldiers about trauma evaluations, suturing, and splinting. In addition, we spent regular time on the shooting range. One of the most intriguing things for me was spending time with the younger guys in the unit. Many of them had questions about relationships, life after deployment, and how to handle *"Dear John letters"* (break-up letters received while on deployment). I had plenty of life experiences to share since I was one of the more senior officers in the unit.

There were plenty of times we received information regarding injuries from firefights. These injuries were quickly managed and the soldiers were shipped out. Iraqi soldiers had a triage facility nearby that was part of our camp. We had actually assisted the Iraqi soldiers in setting up the operations of their clinic. Unfortunately, they rarely used their clinic for patient care instead they routinely came to our clinic for care. Most of the injuries treated in our clinic were manageable, for example we treated isolated fractures, small caliber gunshot wounds and at times an occasional complex hand injury or finger amputation from trauma. We used the medivac choppers regularly to transport patients to Baghdad.

As I mentioned earlier in the book, relationships are so very important. At Camp Hit I had the privilege of meeting Chaplain Captain Terry Partin. He was responsible for the spiritual welfare of our unit. We shared coffee and conversation almost daily. He was a wonderful resource to share private thoughts and to seek wise counsel during stressful times particularly when we had causalities. In November 2005 as we prepared for Thanksgiving our commander was involved in a roadside bomb attack and one of our soldiers was killed. Our commander survived this traumatic event but it significantly affected the morale of our entire unit. The care of our commander and the other soldiers was emotionally draining. It was those times when many of our soldiers sought counsel and a Biblical word from Chaplain Partin to help deal with the loss of our brother in arms. For soldiers killed in combat, we routinely had memorial services honoring the loss of those soldiers.

On a lighter note we worked out by regularly lifting weights and doing cardio on the elliptical. It helped relieve the stress from some of the busy days.

The time at Camp Hit progressed quickly and there were rumors we were going to go home early. I began to ask quiet questions about redeployment and whether I would be returning home with the unit. Our leadership said yes I would be going home with the unit. There was one small thing and that was I couldn't tell my wife when I was coming home. All phone calls coming in and going out of Iraq were monitored and we were forbidden to give out any information about troop movement because the enemy usually has intelligence on us as well. The rumors became true and we were going home a little early in December of 2005. When a unit prepares to leave an area all of the equipment, supplies, and soldiers' personal gear have to be packed. Also one of the most important issues is troop security while we plan for ground transport of the unit.

Once again my stress level was very high due to traveling in an open truck with gear, soldiers, weapons and equipment. Security was one of the most vital points during the travel. We also had to worry about roadside bombs and IEDs. We found a suspected IED and our robot was called to confirm and detonate the bomb. We finally had a sigh of relief once we reached our destination. We were pleased we didn't suffer any troop casualties during our convoy ride from Camp Hit to Baghdad. We were transferred to Balad, Iraq for eventual travel back to Fort Bliss in El Paso, Texas. While at Balad Air Base we were able to finally relax, have a tasty meal, and catch our breath. The best thing occurred when I was able to call home to share the good news with Judi I was coming home. The flight from Balad to Fort Bliss was long and uneventful and we liked it that way. There were no injuries, drama, or problems during the flight. We finally arrived in Fort Bliss to begin the 7 to 10 day redeployment process. We were so excited to be back on American soil and even more excited no one was shooting at us.

Several things took place once we were "squared away". These included turning in your weapon-- any equipment you were issued, and of course an exit physical and mental health exam. Depending on a soldier's Military Occupational Specialty (MOS) some soldiers were involved in direct combat which may have included firefights with the enemy. Other jobs included driving trucks to transport fuel, supplies, or soldiers into hot zones where active firefights were taking place. Because of the trauma associated with war, there is an emotional toll on our soldiers. It may be short-lived after the trauma or it may occur in a delayed manner once soldiers return home from combat.

It was not uncommon for soldiers to contain their private feelings about the things they witnessed or situations they encountered in Iraq. Post-Traumatic Stress Disorder (PTSD) was and is real! For those unfamiliar with PTSD, in the military it is commonly associated with combat-related trauma but we should recognize PTSD can also be associated with non-combat experiences. In combat, soldiers often witness horrific and life-threatening conditions which may consist of the death of a fellow soldier or severe or devastating injuries to soldiers they don't know. I believe all or most soldiers who have been deployed to combat zones have some degree of PTSD. There are so many unpredictable things that happen in war and a soldier can't prepare enough for them all. When you see your battle buddy blown up, and mangled from an IED it almost has to have a lasting effect on the soldier. For our readers who have been exposed to or witnessed gun violence and may have lost friends or loved ones, it's the same. These exposures can cause severe anxiety and stress which is similar to the stress soldiers experience in combat. The traumatic event is the key not necessarily the location of the event. In some of our larger cities in the United States like Chicago, Houston, and Cleveland, shootings seem to occur on a regular basis. But they are not limited to the big cities. We have seen gun violence almost everywhere, including sporting events like football celebrations. Unfortunately, one of the most traumatic events for parents, students and our communities in recent times has been the increase in mass shootings. I hate to think these shootings almost occur several times during the year. One can only imagine the lasting effect of these shootings. However, there have been no real attempts at passing gun legislation despite the number of mass shootings. So, I completely understand the number of people in our society who suffer from PTSD and anxiety not from war combat but from combat in the streets of the United States of America.

When I came home from Iraq for the first time in March 2004, I was definitely affected by my combat experience overseas. Whenever I saw news reports of the war or read newspaper articles about Baghdad, I became extremely emotional for a short period. Emotionally, it seemed as though I was back in Iraq reliving some of my previous experiences. Of course some years after I was home I did speak to a mental health professional who said I didn't have PTSD. I thought I had a mild case of PTSD. Although I did not experience direct combat via a firefight, I did experience the gore and after-effects of it as well as the emotional trauma.

War in itself is traumatic to the human psyche. I clearly remember being awakened by an explosion in January 2004. A vehicle driven by an Iraq civilian was attempting to enter the Green Zone when he detonated a bomb. The bomb exploded killing several soldiers and civilians including people 5 cars behind him. The sound wave traveled nearly one mile and it reverberated the windows in my room. I felt as though the explosion was right outside my door and because of the strength of the explosion I was awakened by the noise of the windows rattling. I immediately jumped on the floor to protect myself. We were unsure if the explosion was incoming or outgoing. Was the explosion caused by us or by the enemy? Following the January 2004 explosion, we had to perform an immediate roll call to account for all the members of our unit. Luckily my unit did not lose any soldiers during that explosion.

Once I returned home from deployment I attended a Cleveland Cavaliers basketball game. Following the introduction of the home team players the Jumbo Tron would spit out fire simulating an explosion. I could barely contain myself and would become jumpy and hypervigilant. Because of my combat experiences in Iraq, I frequently arrive at the Cavaliers games after the start of the game to miss the Jumbo Tron simulated explosion. Also, I no longer attend any 4th of July fireworks because of the loud explosions as you can imagine.

Most, if not all of the soldiers returning from the war were excited about going home and would on occasion withhold information regarding their experiences and their mental health. Any report of significant combat trauma would delay their travel plans and force them to stay at Fort Bliss longer than anticipated.

We were so appreciative of the little things like going out to eat and hanging out with friends once we returned to the Continental United States (CONUS). I was so excited to finally see my family at the Cleveland Hopkins International Airport. I was so excited and happy to see all of them and of course we had a wonderful welcome home party once I returned home.

NOTES

NOTES

CHAPTER FIVE
GROWTH

Temecula is a city north of San Diego by about 70 miles. The population is approximately 110,000 according to the 2020 census. The city is considered inland and is close to the desert. Since Temecula is located close to the desert, the weather is warm most of the time. I was so excited about moving to a community with warm weather.

When Dr. Faerber and I initially began a conversation about possible opportunities to join his practice, I was hesitant about making the decision to move to California. However, I thought I would be a great fit to join his practice and was truly ready for a change.

Judi told me later that leaving Akron Public Schools in January 2006 would result in problems with her retirement pension. So, she said you go ahead and make plans to go to Temecula. We agreed we would travel regularly to see each other on a regular basis. She said that we'll give it a shot and observe how things go, and then at the right time, make arrangements to come join me in Southern California. Unfortunately, I made the move in January 2006 and the transition was not as smooth as I had anticipated. Although I had communicated with the new group when I was moving to Temecula, they did not communicate this to the hospital. When I arrived at the hospital they commented, "We really did not know when you were coming!"

Once I started practicing there-- I was excited and nervous about the new practice, patients, and the local hospitals. I worked at both Inland Valley Medical Center and Riverside County Regional Medical Center, both of which are in Temecula and Moreno Valley, California, which is located approximately 30-40 minutes north of Temecula.

After several weeks I began to tell Judi, I was unhappy with the logistics of the practice. We would have long conversations while I was driving to San Diego to see my brother-in-law and sister-in-law Dale and Lena Kimmey. They made their home in San Diego, California once my brother-in-law retired from the Navy. San Diego, in my opinion is one of the most desirable cities of southern California and the United States except the cost of living is very high. After one such conversation, Judi basically said: "I told you so" which no husband wants to hear of course!

A very intense argument ensued thereafter while en route to San Diego. The stress of the move and the contract issues created significant anxiety at home and I was more concerned about the viability of my marriage compared to practicing in California.

After a tumultuous 5-6 months, I decided that I would come back to Akron to be with my family, particularly since I found out I was having my first grandchild.

Also, one of the more positive experiences was my involvement with the residency training program at Riverside County Regional Medical Center in Moreno Valley, California. This was a level 1 trauma center that served in international community. Approximately 45 to 50% of the patients and/or staff were bilingual. Because of the diverse population, I felt very comfortable in this environment. Even though being away from home was stressful and straining, I needed compensation to support my family. I agreed to continue to work at the County hospital until May 2006. Those 6 months flew by and I became excited about returning to Ohio.

My brother, Artie, flew to San Diego and we started the 2-1/2-day drive back to the Akron area. It was wonderful spending quality time with him. We had quality conversations during our drive and talked about life, his kids and our family. Before I left Southern California, I began to explore other job opportunities in the Midwest and Southeast, including Ohio, Virginia, West Virginia, and South Carolina.

Return to Ohio

I was contacted by a colleague who practiced in a large orthopedic group in Canton, Ohio. They were looking for a hand surgeon. The practice opportunity seemed ideal because of the proximity to home, its unique quality and the partnership opportunities. I felt I would have the opportunity to practice full-time hand surgery in addition to working with a large group with backup coverage. I believe my wife had reconciled the fact we were considering leaving Ohio and pursuing practice opportunities outside of Ohio. I accepted the practice opportunity in Ohio but she was unhappy with my decision to stay in the Akron Canton area. I believe I made this decision because of my comfort of being in this practice location for a number of years and understanding the communities, practice patterns and referral patterns.

In November 2006 I joined Spectrum Orthopedics, a large single specialty group in Canton Ohio. I became a partner a year later and the training seemed to be going smoothly. Because of my previous referrals, I also was asked to come to the Akron area after being contacted by some of my previous patients. Spectrum Orthopedics was agreeable to establishing an office location near Western Reserve Hospital located in Cuyahoga Falls, Ohio. The Cuyahoga Falls branch of my Canton practice grew quickly and 4 years later I made the decision to return full-time back to the Akron area where I could resume teaching orthopedic residents as the orthopedic surgery program director at Western Reserve Hospital. I became a hospital employee and investor at the Western Reserve Hospital in approximately 2010.

Western Reserve Hospital "The New Hospital"

Western Reserve Hospital had previously been Cuyahoga Falls General Hospital, a nonprofit hospital affiliated with Summa Health Systems.

This affiliation with Summa Health Systems occurred in 2001 at which time I was the medical staff president. As medical staff president, I was intimately involved with the merger of Cuyahoga Falls General Hospital and Summa Health System. Western Reserve Hospital became the new entity of a hospital that is owned by a physician for profit. There were local physicians who practiced at Western Reserve Hospital in addition to investors from other community practices. There were several large group practices affiliated with Western Reserve Hospital including Unity Health Network. Ultimately, I transferred my employment to Unity Health Network. Unity Health Network is a large multi-specialty group consisting of primary care, rheumatology, nephrology, pulmonary and infectious disease. I have had a successful practice in this location since coming back to Ohio. Once I made the decision to return to Western Reserve Hospital, I was asked to reconsider taking on the position of program director for the Orthopedic Surgery Residency Program. I was asked to assume the leadership of the program because of my reputation, respect and commitment to education. In 2017, during a meeting with the CEO of Western Reserve Hospital, I was asked to consider the leadership role of Chairman of the

Dept. of Surgery which oversees all of the surgical divisions. After deliberation, I accepted the position of Chairman of the Dept. of Surgery. The position has been time consuming but rewarding most of the time because it allows me to participate in the leadership of the hospital and interact with division and other department leaders.

My orthopedic practice is still busy with referrals from a number of providers. My practice has been successful because we provide quality and compassionate care. I believe all physicians should provide quality, compassionate care but some miss this mark. Being a physician is a calling but unfortunately, many physicians forget one small thing which is the ability to listen with empathy. The care of patients should be predicated on **compassion, affordability**, and **high quality**. No matter your chosen profession, remember the golden rule which says *to treat people the way you want to be treated.* I would also add develop the ability to not only hear but to listen and develop a high-quality work ethic. I believe the COVID-19 epidemic was a significant factor affecting the quality of patient care rendered in hospitals. In addition, COVID-19 affected our workforce due to layoffs, terminations and loss of hospital revenue. All of these factors appeared to cause the great resignation in 2020 and 2021 which affected the number and the quality of workers. The decline in the quality of workers, combined with the demand of rising salaries and the increase in traveling workers contributed to declining revenues for hospitals as well as other industries.

For young people entering college, trade school or the workforce-- as the great golfer Tiger Woods would say "Bring your 'A' game every day." Do you think you can do that? I am sure you can!

Education and Mentoring

Educating and mentoring are about empowering and enlightening our students and residents to pursue their dreams and reach for the stars. I'm honored to be a role model for those in training to model excellence. Dedication is required to become a great physician and an educator. At times, I believe some of the students underestimate the **time commitment** and **dedication** required to become an excellent physician. It is commonly believed that anyone can be average or low. In medicine I feel there is no room to be limited. Think about it! Do you want an average or low heart surgeon performing open heart surgery on your parents or would you want a low spine surgeon performing a major spine procedure on your grandfather or grandmother? We should all strive for excellence regardless of what specialty we choose. It takes years to complete undergraduate studies and medical school with excellent grades. Once you become a physician in training the pursuit of excellence must continue. For more than thirty years I've had the pleasure of mentoring, and teaching medical students and orthopedic residents. I've also had the privilege of influencing their personal, professional and educational growth in the course of their journey to become physicians and surgeons.

I receive great joy in watching the transformation of a shy, reserved third or fourth year medical student ready to take on the world once they graduate from medical school and prepare for the next phase of their journey. I fondly remember a recent graduate of our program who did not get into medical school on the first attempt. I had conversations with him to reassure him he would be accepted into medical school. As one can imagine, he also possessed a moderate degree of anxiety during the application process. He was accepted into medical school the following year and was chosen as the top choice for our orthopedic residency. I've been able to mentor him during the residency program and he has become an excellent surgeon. We met regularly to ensure he was progressing satisfactorily and to address any concerns that surfaced. It has been an honor to watch him grow from medical school through his residency. He is now prepared to pursue a post-graduate fellowship in a highly competitive orthopedic sub-specialty.

In 2017 after becoming chairman of the department of surgery, I considered it another opportunity to impact our hospital as their leader in addition to my role as orthopedic surgery division chief and residency director. Becoming Chairman of the Department of Surgery involves charge of the various divisions in our surgical department. These included Orthopedics, Anesthesia, ENT or

Ear Nose and Throat, General & Plastic Surgery, Neurosurgery, Urogynecology & Gynecology, Plastics and Endoscopy.

In addition to my role as chairman, my role as orthopedic surgery program director involves a significant amount of my time as well. I am responsible for the charge of the orthopedic surgery residency, making sure we follow the guidelines of the American Council for Graduate Medical Education (ACGME) which is the accrediting body for all postgraduate programs in medical education. In my role as a program director, I am responsible for making sure the residents have adequate surgical experiences-- in all sub-specialties of orthopedic surgery as well as making sure they make satisfactory progress in those respective rotations. Ultimately our goal is to successfully train and graduate orthopedic residents after 5 years of residency who are competent and safe to practice their craft. Approximately 90 percent of our graduates pursue post-graduate fellowship specialty training in sub-specialties including pediatrics, sports medicine, spine surgery as well as total joint surgery, shoulder, hand & upper extremity reconstruction.

It gives me great joy to teach and motivate ambitious, inquisitive, third and fourth year medical students to strive for excellence. I love to see the spark in their eyes when they answer a question correctly or discuss a challenging topic from beginning to end. Once a student graduates from medical school he or she becomes a resident physician during the next phase of their journey. Residency training is time consuming, and challenging with an increasing level of responsibilities regardless of the length of training. If the residents are married and have children, their challenges can be even greater. I often say the residents are like teenage children; they have different personalities and work ethics. In the last 5-10 years I have observed the residents' approach to clinical scenarios and decision making. I often think they don't approach patients the way I did and of course this is a bit egotistical to think they would approach patients and decision making the same way I did. Of course I finished my training more than 30 years ago. But remember there is always room for high quality, compassionate care for all patients regardless of their situation or their ability to pay.

The residents have to be molded into excellent physicians and surgeons and their growth and development can take several years after graduating from medical school. In general, the medicine residencies are shorter than the surgical residencies. Family Medicine, Internal Medicine, and Emergency Medicine all require 3 years of post-graduate training. Most surgical residencies are 4-8 years depending on the specialty. A residency in Obstetrics and Gynecology requires 4 post-graduate years of training compared to Orthopedics which requires 5 years of training. To become a plastic, cardiac, or neurosurgeon it can take an additional 7-8 years of post-graduate training after medical school.

NOTES

NOTES

CHAPTER SIX
THE JOURNEY

In addition to learning medicine and orthopedic surgery, residents must learn to work in teams and trust one another. On occasion I use the analogy of Navy Seals when describing the most effective and efficient residents. The Navy Seals are named after the environment in which they serve: The Sea, Air and Land. The seals operate in small groups with a singular purpose to complete the mission without losing fellow seals, making them highly organized and efficient. In comparison, the orthopedic surgery residents must work together in small groups with the goal of providing high quality patient care, and assisting fellow residents in ensuring patient safety. If our residents are not trustworthy and reliable this can cause trust and morale issues amongst the group and the faculty.

The faculty's goal is to teach, motivate and transform residents into fully trained board eligible or certified orthopedic surgeons over 5 years. I have been involved in medical education for close to 30 years and it has been extremely rewarding. I am proud to have motivated, influenced, guided and educated our students and residents to become excellent physicians and surgeons. I feel honored to educate and mentor young people because many years ago someone recognized something special in me and gave me an opportunity to pursue my dream of becoming a surgeon. Many medical students complete their third and fourth years of clinical training at our hospital. Our hospital is a major training site for students from The Ohio University Heritage College of Osteopathic Medicine (OU-HCOM).

The Ohio University Heritage College of Osteopathic Medicine has three campuses: they are located in Athens, Dublin and Cleveland. The Dublin campus partnered with Ohio Health which is a large health system that owns several hospitals in the central Ohio region. They have a Diversity Scholars Program which focuses on recruiting and retaining under-represented minority students to practice with Ohio Health in Central Ohio or other surrounding communities. The Cleveland campus is partnered with the renowned Cleveland Clinic Foundation. They also have a Diversity Scholars Program and they are committed to educating and recruiting physicians for Northeast Ohio. I have had the pleasure of mentoring students from both the Cleveland and Dublin campuses. I meet with the students monthly for breakfast or coffee to review their progress, discuss any challenges if any, and provide guidance when necessary. I get as much joy as the students when I can tell they are figuring things out and becoming successful on their rotations.

One of the greatest moments for me is when graduation finally arrives and I can 'hood' them on stage as part of the graduation ceremony. Many of my patients have made positive comments regarding my gift of being a great teacher and mentor. Finally, when the new resident physician arrives at the hospital "green" and doesn't know anything, he or she rotates with our orthopedic department faculty on the various sub-specialty services during their 5years of training. After successful completion of their training program, they are ready to practice or pursue further training and I feel satisfied my job is done!

For our aspiring students, regardless of where you are in your journey, make sure you have a mentor in your corner or someone you can go to for advice and guidance about your educational journey.

Shadowing (following and observing) someone while in high school is a wonderful opportunity to see firsthand what a person does at work. He or she may have an interesting job that you haven't thought of. Students should be sure to ask plenty of questions-- for example what mentors like and don't like about their jobs. No matter how old you are, don't be afraid to ask your mentor about his or her journey. Who knows, your mentor may have had challenges as well!

When I was in medical school, I asked my mentor about his performance in Biochemistry. He responded, "You don't need an excellent Biochemistry score to become an orthopedic surgeon."

His comments gave me the encouragement and confidence I needed to successfully complete Biochemistry. For the most part, your mentor will listen and glean from your conversation exactly what you need and provide the appropriate words of guidance and encouragement.

I think my lifelong lessons for the students regarding mentoring would be:

- Find a mentor early in your journey and establish a good relationship with them.
- Don't be afraid to ask questions about the mentor's journey.
- There are no dumb questions.
- Think about shadowing your mentor or someone in the field you're considering.
- Meet with your mentor on a regular basis for example monthly meetings or weekly emails or texting.

Leadership and Giving Back

New Hope Baptist Church gave me the opportunity to learn leadership as a young person. I often wondered why I gravitated towards leadership. There is research to suggest sibling position may be a strong predictor of leadership. More specifically, the oldest child often gravitates towards leadership positions and the younger siblings tend to be followers. It makes perfect sense to me because I'm the oldest sibling and had to babysit or watch the kids while mom and/or dad were at work. Therefore, I missed out on sports and other high school activities because of family commitments and responsibilities as a young leader.

In contrast to my younger brothers, who both played sports—one played football and the other played baseball. Leadership was not a requirement for them. Due to being the oldest sibling, we are often expected to lead. It was about the responsibility and expectation of doing your part in helping the family. The tone was set by our parents and the oldest siblings to embrace the responsibility of leadership although that was not our intention in the beginning. For example, I often observe my grandson Kaiden and his relationship with his sisters: Sania who is 2 years younger and Amina who is 8 years younger. His behavior and conversation are very similar to mine when I was his age. Even at church he is slowly becoming a consistent helper and junior leader in Sunday school. We recently had a vacation Bible school and I received wonderful comments about my grandson's spirit and his willingness to help in all aspects of the activities. Have you ever thought about why you are a leader? Perhaps, now the answer makes sense.

As I mentioned in one of the earlier chapters, there was an expectation in my household and our church for young people to become actively involved in church. This involvement helps to provide the template for leadership and life which is crucial for working with people from different backgrounds and dealing with different situations. There are several qualities necessary to become a successful leader.

These include the following: *Respect, Integrity, Interpersonal Communication, Responsibility and Reliability, Humility and Adaptivity.* Early in life I learned the importance of *Respect, Integrity and Interpersonal Communication.* These fundamental qualities of effective leadership were modeled by our pastor and other leaders at the church. Respect is a fundamental quality that should be shown by all leaders. It is a basic concept that suggests we *treat people like we want to be treated.* This trait of leadership will carry you throughout your life.

Interpersonal Communication is also required to be an effective leader. There are meetings, lectures, and public presentations where effective communication is necessary to relay your message. In most if not all employment situations, one will be required to effectively communicate with your customers, co-workers and supervisors. In healthcare for example, one has to effectively communicate with patients, medical and nursing staff, and hospital leaders. Effective interpersonal communication is really about hearing, listening and understanding the things necessary for you to connect with team members. A leader's ability to hear and listen will allow him or her to be receptive to the ideas of others.

One of the most important characteristics of effective leadership is **Integrity**. This involves *honesty and reliability.* It boils down to this: *can we trust or believe what you say?* Another way of looking at integrity is: *will he or she do the right thing when no one is looking?* Your word is your bond and this is a major determinant of your character.

Next, let's look at **Humility**. Some people in the professional world view humility as *strength, not being boastful or haughty.* Humble leaders listen more and acknowledge others more than themselves. This allows others to grow, and become more comfortable, which will prepare them for leadership roles in the future.

Although there are probably more qualities of effective leaders, the last one I will discuss is **Adaptivity**. This quality involves being able to receive information from your team, other leaders as well as some of your co-workers. In addition, adaptivity means being able to receive, process information, and make crucial and sometimes not so popular decisions about the direction of the organization. One of the most common examples is having to make tough decisions relative to layoffs. When the expenses of an organization go up and revenues are down, at times difficult decisions have to be made to make sure the loss of revenue is reversed. This may require layoffs which can be life changing and in some cases devastating.

While a member of a hospital committee and a member of a national board, I learned how the members interact, how the chairman or president conducts the meeting and how decisions are made. In addition, I became involved in medical school committee work which ultimately works on behalf of our medical school and their students.

When I returned from my first tour in Iraq, I became interested in Health Policy. Health Policy is involved with policy making as it relates to Graduate Medical Educations, and CMS (Centers for Medicare and Medicaid Services) which deals with covering the salaries and benefits for residents in training programs and how bills drafted in Congress become laws.

In addition, we also studied how funding works for underserved and underrepresented communities. More specifically, how the underserved and underinsured receive high-quality, affordable, and compassionate care. We visited 9-10 Osteopathic Medical Schools across the country where we had monthly graduate-level classes for 11 months. The classes were held on Friday, Saturday, and Sunday. In 2005, I completed a Health Policy Fellowship through Ohio University Heritage College of Osteopathic Medicine (OU-HCOM) and the New York Institute of Technology/New York College of Osteopathic Medicine under the leadership of Barbara Ross-Lee, D.O. At the time of the fellowship, Dr. Ross-Lee was the dean at OU-HCOM in Athens, Ohio. In our Health Policy program these qualities of leadership were emphasized. Some of these included *Interpersonal Communication, Collaboration, Integrity, Respect and Empathy.* I was able to apply what I had learned in the Health Policy

Program to my work on committees at our hospital, medical school, and the American Osteopathic Academy of Orthopedics.

OU-HCOM Society and Friends

For example, in my role as president of the Society of Alumni & Friends at OU-HCOM, I represented our medical school and alumni at local, state and national levels. In addition, I earned the trust and respect of our board members which helped me become a better leader. There were often challenging decisions to be made regarding policies and procedures and the best way to engage alumni to return to campus and support the college with their *time, talent* and *treasure*. I needed the support of the board to make sure the Society of Alumni Friends was successful.

NOTES

CHAPTER SEVEN

LEADERS ARE MENTORS

There will be times in your life when you are the mentee and other times when you pay it forward. Investing your time and wisdom in others is a core quality of a natural leader.

In addition to serving on the board of the Society of Alumni & Friends, I have been blessed to be on several boards throughout my career and some of these include Past President and Board Director of The American Osteopathic Academy of Orthopedics which represents over 3 thousand orthopedic surgeons; Trustee of the Ohio University Foundation, the fundraising arm of the University; Trustee for the Ohio Osteopathic Society which is the state medical society for osteopathic physicians in the state of Ohio. All of these boards have given me a wonderful opportunity to serve and give back to various communities.

The other point I want to emphasize is the *significance of giving back.* I feel I have been blessed to make a difference in the lives of my patients, students, residents and friends on 'our' journey. For students or readers going through challenging times be it classes, family, relationships or finances it is so important to recognize your blessing and how someone has said a prayer for you, given you wise counsel, and encouraged you when you had no more energy in the tank. There are people out there who believe in you.

Don't let yourself believe you don't have anything to give back, because you do. Individuals who give back to communities have such a sense of purpose and are often happier, less stressed, and feel blessed themselves. Through my 30 years as a surgeon, I am convinced that my gift of service and excellent care to those patients has resulted in improved lives and a return to activities they enjoy. My gift of service was evident regardless of whether it was treatment abroad during Operation Iraqi Freedom or here locally in my orthopedic practice in Cuyahoga Falls. I treated soldiers in Iraq with devastating injuries, some of which left them with permanent deformities and disabilities. While in Iraq I felt that I was doing a significant amount of work to care for our soldiers, either return them to battle or send them back to the United States for further care. My experiences caring for Mr. Weisskopf and James Beverly in particular were life altering. I felt I was there for that special time and they needed my expertise. Especially Mr. Weisskopf who suffered a significant blast injury to his hand.

Mr. Beverly was a soldier from the Akron area who was injured in the same explosion as Mr. Weisskopf. Meeting someone from Akron really made him more comfortable. Regarding Mr.

Weisskopf, despite the significance of his devastating injury I was able to assure him things were going to be okay and he would be able to care for his daughter once he was in Washington, D.C.

It's about caring for patients and returning them to function. I have treated patients with a multitude of problems and some of these are fractures or broken bones, severe arthritis of the hands or shoulders, and chronic nerve and tendon injuries. We have a satisfied customer once we alleviate pain and restore their ability to resume activity. All in all, I feel like I'm giving back to my community with my talent and treasure. In **1 Peter 4:10** (NIV) It reads, *"Each of you should use whatever gift you have received to serve others, as faithful stewards of God's grace in its various forms"*

You don't have to be a surgeon if that's not your gift. Perhaps you're an aspiring teacher, accountant, police officer, firefighter or nurse. As the scripture reads, we all have our unique gifts. For my readers, whatever your gift is please give it your best and think about how you can help others. Hopefully, this will resonate with my readers and you will be motivated to excel and strive for excellence. Remember that it's possible to use your gifts to bless others. I've been reminded of my blessing since I started college in 1974.

If you're lucky enough to have had a mentor, you know how valuable they are.

Let's take a quick look at some of the few people who have impacted my life. The Reverend Gerald Jackson was a chemical engineer who worked at Goodyear Tire and Rubber Co. He was also the Children's Church pastor at New Hope Baptist Church, Akron, Ohio. He was instrumental in helping me navigate challenges with inorganic chemistry; Mrs. Mary Burner, R.N., my Medical Careers Director and teacher at John R. Buchtel High School who saw something special in me and instilled confidence in me regarding my abilities; Steve Hilliard, PhD, professor of Biology and my advisor at Baldwin Wallace University (formerly Baldwin Wallace College) who consistently encouraged and advised me to apply to Ohio University Heritage College of Osteopathic Medicine (OU-HCOM) and drove me to Athens, Ohio to check out the program; Jules Glover, D.O., an osteopathic primary care physician who was kind enough to write a letter of recommendation for me to attend the OU-HCOM; Frank C. Forshew, M.D., hand surgeon and mentor who employed me during my gap year before I started medical school and was a great resource about medical school, orthopedics and hand surgery. My mother, Doretta L. Dunkley consistently encouraged, supported and reinforced the notion I could do all things in Christ if I was prepared when the opportunity presented itself. The Reverend John H. Flinn, my first pastor of The New Hope Baptist Church, Akron, Ohio who modeled leadership, service and integrity. The Reverend Theodore DeWitt Smith who succeeded pastor Flinn. Pastor Smith reinforced the importance of education, striving for excellence, and giving back to our community.

I could go on and on but there were a multitude of people who have impacted my journey.

Being the recipient of such a blessing in my life compelled me to make a difference in the lives of young people. Those young people aspiring to become medical students and physicians or those who want a better life and want to go to college but don't have the funds or anyone to support them are the people I'm committed to mentoring and coaching.

Letter to You, the Reader

Lessons Learned

In my opinion, all of my collective experiences contributed to the physician, surgeon, educator, mentor and leader I am today. Little did I know those early church leadership exposures, including public speaking would be pivotal in all aspects of my professional career. Also, close working relationships and professional experiences have prepared me for leadership positions on national boards and trustee positions, and as mentioned earlier, president of the medical staff, program director and chairman of the department of surgery at Western Reserve Hospital.

The message that will resonate with you, the reader is *early exposure and success in academics, finding a mentor that you can trust and developing a solid working relationship* with him or her. If you do these things, when financial challenges present themselves-- perhaps you doubt your abilities and you lack support, you still have a wonderful opportunity to achieve your dreams!

For you, the reader, decide to choose to be different, more focused and prepare for life with intentionality. In our country, we tend to rely on information given to us by a host of individuals without doing our due diligence or our research. Without investigating the information, we may be presented with false information resulting in a scam. It is vitally important to seek knowledge and not solely rely on your friends who are generally uninformed.

Many of your so-called friends will be jealous of your success and try to derail your progress. Some of these individuals are not your friends at all. In an earlier chapter I said all kids really want is to be accepted and to be liked. Remember this, after high school many of those same people will move away and you will not have any contact with them for the rest of their lives. Keep in mind that not all people have good intentions for you.

In high school, students should ask counselors and teachers tough questions about career choices and scholarship opportunities. If you try hard and apply for almost every scholarship you may be able to have a lot of tuition covered. Perhaps you question how will you pay for college or which college you want to attend? The answer should be a college that gives you the most money or the college that I can afford. It is okay to attend community college for the first 2 years especially if you don't know what you want to study. Then transfer to a 4 year institution once your finances are better and your mind is made up about what to study.

Many years ago at our home church, the Arlington Church of God taught us a simple acronym that could help keep your life on the straight and narrow. The acronym is **L.I.F.E.** It reads *'life'* when you look at the letters collectively.

L is for **Love.** The universal language and expression for one to another. It can also be a *strong interest* or pleasure like that of a basketball or football team, or sport such as golf. Many years ago, a group called the Beatles sang a song entitled *"All You Need Is Love"* If you remember this basic principle, then you have done your part. It is the fundamental way of how we should treat people that we encounter day in and day out.

I stands for **Integrity**. The quality of being honest and doing the right thing when no one is looking. It is also described as *moral uprightness*. Integrity is something good leaders will consistently show in all they do. Integrity is akin to character.

F stands for **Faith.** A *strong belief* in something with or without the evidence to support the belief. Earlier in this book I referred to *Faith* that was demonstrated many times throughout my life, particularly early when applying to medical school. My faith was crucial during my deployments twice to Iraq in a combat zone, where I was in danger and hoped to return home safely. If we convince ourselves to believe something, it is possible we can achieve whatever we want backed with diligence.

E is for **Excellence**. The quality of being *outstanding* or extremely good. There is no room for mediocrity. Striving for excellence will open doors for you professionally or personally. Consider achieving high grades, which will open up new academic opportunities and prepare you for the unknown. Excellence in sports may assist you in receiving a college scholarship. My commitment to excellence as a surgeon has allowed me to have a successful 30-year orthopedic surgery practice. Consider this, everyone admires the valedictorian because of his or her academic excellence. Most of us only wish we were the valedictorian of our high school.

I would like to share with you another example of excellence: My wife and I serve on the Congressional Military Academy Appointment Committee for Senators from Ohio. The committee has the responsibility to interview students who are applying to the Military Academy such as The United States Military Academy at West Point, Air Force Academy, Naval Academy, and the Merchant Marines. All of the students are accomplished academically, athletically and civically. Many of the students interviewed have grade point averages well above the standard 4.0 scale. I have always been impressed when I see a high school student with a GPA of 4.0 or greater. This means that they have taken all honors and/or advanced placement classes. My wife and I are so impressed and honored to be a part of an important process. The students represent our best and brightest and many of them will be future leaders of our country.

Looking back on My Journey

I'd love to conclude by sharing some personal experiences about my journey. I'd like to reflect on some important decisions that affected my path. In high school I knew I wanted to become a physician but did not have a clear understanding of the requirements to complete the journey. My journey was almost derailed because of finances and lack of confidence. Being a first-generation college and medical school graduate, there were several experiences with family that impacted my financial life. These include decision making, having a plan and sticking to the plan regardless of the obstacles. The decision to divorce, for example, had a significant impact on professional opportunities. These included returning to Akron to begin my practice and not pursuing other job opportunities outside of the Akron area. I committed to being in the Akron area because being a good dad required me to be present! Adjustments were made in my career and I have been extremely satisfied with my professional and family life.

My family was so proud of me becoming a doctor. They treated me as though I was the bank for the family. Our home was the location for most holiday celebrations. In addition, my wife and I proudly helped my mother whose only source of income was social security in retirement. We both felt it was the least we could do. When you achieve success, keep in mind that your family and friends may turn to you for financial assistance. Now of course there were things I could have done better like saving and investing. I took trips with children and bought them nearly everything I could imagine. To me there was so much joy in being able to provide a better life or experience for them. I'm wondering if their life was better than mine.

When I started practice at age thirty-six, I was already behind the eight ball when it came to savings and investing. Of course I made gains because my salary are higher than the general public. I had significant student loan debt and other expenses to manage. I felt I had to have a strategy to quickly eliminate my debt. I was able to negotiate my student loan repayment for a commitment to practice in Akron community. This decision was pivotal in eliminating the bulk of my debt. Students, for example, need to be *intentional about a plan* for their lives and avoid spontaneous random decisions that can have a significant impact on their future. In some sense of the word, I think I should have had a better plan. In reality perhaps a plan would've been helpful. Having a plan provides structure and discipline to your life and helps your decision making and accountability.

When I first went into practice 30 years ago retirement seemed so far away, however, the years flew by. I practiced at North Star Orthopedics for 13 years and my practice was disrupted twice by deploying to Iraq. Those 2 deployments had a significant impact on my finances and my ability to save and invest for the future. I think I should've listened more carefully and sought out wise counsel. After my deployment, I moved to California for 6 months for a new job opportunity that didn't work. I joined a practice in Canton Ohio for 4 years only to return to Akron to finish my career.

The question is often asked: "Would you do it again (become a surgeon)?" The answer is: "Yes, maybe differently but yes I would!" I have been practicing for thirty plus years now, and it has been the culmination of living a dream. My advice to you would be to chase your dreams hard and never give up.

Overall, I'm very proud of my accomplishments, career and the number of lives I've impacted. I feel God has blessed me with a gift to make a difference in the lives of so many people including my patients, children, grandchildren, veterans, journalists and many others. When I retire, I want to be known as **a man who loved God, and his family, was a great husband, father and grandfather, who touched the lives of so many, and hopefully made this world a better place!**

Your future is in your hands!

Made in United States
Orlando, FL
20 May 2024

47071580R00078